E.B. White

WHO WROTE THAT?

E.B. White

Aimee LaBrie

Foreword by
Kyle Zimmer

CHELSEA HOUSE
PUBLISHERS
A Haights Cross Communications Company ®

Philadelphia

CHELSEA HOUSE PUBLISHERS

VP, NEW PRODUCT DEVELOPMENT Sally Cheney
DIRECTOR OF PRODUCTION Kim Shinners
CREATIVE MANAGER Takeshi Takahashi
MANUFACTURING MANAGER Diann Grasse

STAFF FOR E.B. WHITE

EXECUTIVE EDITOR Matt Uhler
EDITORIAL ASSISTANT Sarah Sharpless
PRODUCTION EDITOR Noelle Nardone
PHOTO EDITOR Sarah Bloom
SERIES DESIGNER Keith Trego
LAYOUT 21st Century Publishing and Communications, Inc.

A Haights Cross Communications ✦ Company ®

First Printing

1 3 5 7 9 8 6 4 2

Library of Congress Cataloging-in-Publication Data

LaBrie, Aimee, 1969–
  E.B. White/Aimee LaBrie.
    p. cm.
Includes bibliographical references.
  ISBN 0-7910-8235-0 (alk. paper)
  1. White, E. B. (Elwyn Brooks), 1899- 2. Authors, American—20th century—
Biography. I. Title.
PS3545.H5187Z74 2004
818'.5209—dc22

                                        2004022579

All links and Web addresses were checked and verified to be correct at the time
of publication. Because of the dynamic nature of the Web, some addresses
and links may have changed since publication and may no longer be valid.

Table of Contents

FOREWORD BY
KYLE ZIMMER
PRESIDENT, FIRST BOOK

HUMANITY IS POWERED by stories. From our earliest days as thinking beings, we employed every available tool to tell each other stories. We danced, drew pictures on the walls of our caves, spoke, and sang. All of this extraordinary effort was designed to entertain, recount the news of the day, explain natural occurrences—and then gradually to build religious and cultural traditions and establish the common bonds and continuity that eventually formed civilizations. Stories are the most powerful force in the universe; they are the primary element that has distinguished our evolutionary path.

Our love of the story has not diminished with time. Enormous segments of societies are devoted to the art of storytelling. Book sales in the United States alone topped $26 billion last year; movie studios spend fortunes to create and promote stories; and the news industry is more pervasive in its presence than ever before.

There is no mystery to our fascination. Great stories are magic. They can introduce us to new cultures, or remind us of the nobility and failures of our own, inspire us to greatness or scare us to death; but above all, stories provide human insight on a level that is unavailable through any other source. In fact, stories connect each of us to the rest of humanity not just in our own time, but also throughout history.

This special magic of books is the greatest treasure that we can hand down from generation to generation. In fact, that spark in a child that comes from books became the motivation for the creation of my organization, First Book, a national literacy program with a simple mission: to provide new books to the most disadvantaged children. At present, First Book has been at work in hundreds of communities for over a decade. Every year children in need receive millions of books through our organization and millions more are provided through dedicated literacy institutions across the United States and around the world. In addition, groups of people dedicate themselves tirelessly to working with children to share reading and stories in every imaginable setting from schools to the streets. Of course, this Herculean effort serves many important goals. Literacy translates to productivity and employability in life and many other valid and even essential elements. But at the heart of this movement are people who love stories, love to read, and want desperately to ensure that no one misses the wonderful possibilities that reading provides.

When thinking about the importance of books, there is an overwhelming urge to cite the literary devotion of great minds. Some have written of the magnitude of the importance of literature. Amy Lowell, an American poet, captured the concept with her statement when she said, "Books are more than books. They are the life, the very heart and core of ages past, the reason why men lived and worked and died, the essence and quintessence of their lives." Others have spoken of their personal obsession with books, as in Thomas Jefferson's simple statement: "I live for books." But more compelling, perhaps, is the almost instinctive excitement in children for books and stories.

Throughout my years at First Book, I have heard truly extraordinary stories about the power of books in the lives of children. In one case, a homeless child, who had been bounced from one location to another, later resurfaced—and the only possession that he had fought to keep was the book he was given as part of a First Book distribution months earlier. More recently, I met a child who, upon receiving the book he wanted, flashed a big smile and said, "This is my big chance!" These snapshots reveal the true power of books and stories to give hope and change lives.

As these children grow up and continue to develop their love of reading, they will owe a profound debt to those volunteers who reached out to them—a debt that they may repay by reaching out to spark the next generation of readers. But there is a greater debt owed by all of us—a debt to the storytellers, the authors, who have bound us together, inspired our leaders, fueled our civilizations, and helped us put our children to sleep with their heads full of images and ideas.

WHO WROTE THAT? is a series of books dedicated to introducing us to a few of these incredible individuals. While we have almost always honored stories, we have not uniformly honored storytellers. In fact, some of the most important authors have toiled in complete obscurity throughout their lives or have been openly persecuted for the uncomfortable truths that they have laid before us. When confronted with the magnitude of their written work or perhaps the daily grind of our own, we can forget that writers are people. They struggle through the same daily indignities and dental appointments, and they experience the intense joy and bottomless despair that many of us do. Yet somehow they rise above it all to deliver a powerful thread that connects us all. It is a rare honor to have the opportunity that these books provide to share the lives of these extraordinary people. Enjoy.

E.B. White as an infant, surrounded by his father, mother, and sister Marion (top row), and siblings Lillian, Albert, Stanley, and Clara (bottom row). Though often surrounded by a busy family life, as the youngest of six children, White often felt alone. At the age of eight years old, he began writing in his journal, perhaps to ease his loneliness. It was a habit that he would keep all of his life.

1

The Great Outdoors

IT STARTED WITH a mouse.

When Elwyn Brooks White was a child, he would lay in the dark under the covers of his quilt, listening to the sounds of the mice scrambling inside the walls of his bedroom at 101 Summit Avenue in Mount Vernon, New York. Rather than being frightened, White found something comforting about knowing that the mice were going on about their business, not bothering him, but not running away in fear either. When he was nine years old, he even composed a poem for his older brother Stanley entitled "A Story of a Little Mouse":

Once there was a wise little mouse
At least that's what he thought,
But this experience shows you
Just what his wisdom brought.

One day he walked through the kitchen
A wire box he spied
And in it was a hunk of cheese
Which he very carefully eyed.

Then he decided he'd have some
So in the box he stepped
Farther and farther and farther
Very cautiously he crept.

But all of a sudden the trap sprang
And cut right off his head.
That cruel trap had been laid for him
And there he lay quite dead.

As a lesson for a little mouse
I certainly advise
That mice had better be careful,
And not try to be too wise.

A few months later, this same poem won him a prize in 1909 from *Woman's Home Companion*. As an adult, he would remember the fondness he felt for these foragers. This admiration blossomed into his first children's book, *Stuart Little*, an adventure story about one courageous boy mouse who lived with a family in New York before setting out on his own in a miniature Model-T Ford.

From the beginning of his life, White loved animals and everything associated with the outdoors. Though he and his family lived in the tree-lined suburbs of New York, they did have a large lawn and a barn. At one time or another, White raised pigeons, chameleons, polliwogs, caterpillars, turtles, and canaries. The family always had a dog on hand who White could take along when he went foraging under fallen tree branches for bugs or lizards. White loved his first dog, a collie named Mac, so much that he built him a sheepskin-lined home in the barn to keep the dog warm during icy winter nights. He remembers Mac fondly, and his own anxiety about the dog's happiness:

> I can still see my first dog in all the moods and situations that memory has filed him away in, but I think of him oftenest as he used to be right after breakfast on the back porch, list-lessly eating up a dish of petrified oatmeal rather than hurt my feelings. For six years he met me at the same place after school and convoyed me home—a service he thought up himself. A boy doesn't forget that sort of association.[1]

While Mount Vernon offered a taste of the country life, the house was just a twenty-five-minute train ride into Grand Central Station in New York, where one could be made dizzy by the skyscrapers, the calling of street vendors, and the exhilarating crush of people crowding the sidewalks. For White, the bustle of city life captivated him as much as the hum of the cicadas outside his bed-room window. Throughout his lifetime, White continued to be torn between city and country life. While he thrived on the energy in Manhattan, it could also overwhelm him. In later years, he more than once left a job to return to a calmer life in the countryside.

Elwyn Brooks White came into the world on July 11, 1899, the last of six children of Jessica Hart White and Samuel Tilly White, both of whom were born in Brooklyn. At the time White was born, his mother was forty-one and his father was forty-five. His father started working at Waters Piano Company at age thirteen and eventually became president of the business. White's mother descended from Scottish ancestry. Her father, William Hart, was a well-known landscape painter who was one of the first members of the Hudson River School in New York. Jessica Hart White was a kind, if somewhat frail woman, who may have passed on some of her bashfulness to her son as well as her interest in the outdoors. To be sure, White admired and loved his mother. In fact, he dedicated his first book of poems to her. When White was born, his sisters, Marion, Clara, and Lillian, were aged eighteen, fifteen, and five, respectively, and his brothers, Albert and Stanley, were eleven and eight. Of all his siblings, White was closest to Stanley. After Stanley left home to attend Cornell University, White wrote him letters which he jokingly signed "Master Elwyn Brooks White" or "Buttercup."

The house in which White lived was never short on liveliness. Because his father worked with pianos (and even had a few of his musical compositions published), the house was filled with instruments: pianos, violins, bongos, trumpets, and a viola, among others. The family would occasionally put on impromptu (if not very musically appealing) concerts. White tried learning the mandolin, cello, and piano, and though he did managed to develop a serious crush on his piano teacher, Miss Ihlefeld, he never learned to do more than play a few off-key notes.

Though his childhood was secure and full of things he loved—ice-skating in the winter at a nearby pond, and bicycling and canoeing during the summer—Elwyn found himself troubled at times by questions bigger than himself:

> As a child, I was frightened but not unhappy. I lacked for nothing except confidence. I suffered nothing except the routine terrors of childhood: fear of the dark, fear of the future, fear of the return to school after a summer on a lake in Maine, fear of making an appearance on a platform, fear of the lavatory in the school basement where the slate urinals cascaded, fear that I was unknowing about things I should know about.[2]

Not all writers are troubled or come from unhappy homes, but White, though frequently in the midst of the hustle and bustle of his family, often felt alone. In part to understand and heal this sense of isolation, he turned toward writing. At the early age of eight, he began keeping a journal, a habit he continued for the rest of his days. When he was older, White would sometimes open up one of these old journals, the pages yellowed and the ink faded, to remember the boy he once had been.

White showed an early affection for words. Before he even set foot in Public School 2 on Lincoln Avenue, his older brother Stanley taught White how to sound out words by giving him copies of *The New York Times* newspaper. White loved to run his index finger down the columns, even if, at the age of six, he didn't quite understand the definitions. He learned later to appreciate the precise meanings of words from his father, who would send his children up to Albert's room to page through *Webster's Unabridged Dictionary* when they didn't use a word properly.

Though he enjoyed words, White tolerated, but did not love, school. He feared any type of public speaking, he didn't like to read, and he only finished his homework because he was afraid of getting in trouble with his teachers. He longed to get away from the desks that were bolted to the floor and to sled down a hill on a slick patch of ice or chase bullfrogs through the tall weeds behind his house. He continued to write for his own pleasure, and his first short story, a tale of a dog named Don, was published in a well-known children's journal, *St. Nicholas Magazine*, when he was eleven years old. He won the coveted gold medal from the same magazine three years later for a similar story about an adventurous dog entitled "A True Dog Story."

In an essay called "A Boy I Knew," White refers to himself in the third person, describing how, as a child, Sunday

Did you know...

The first ten years of E.B. White's childhood saw the following new inventions and innovations: the first motor-powered vacuum cleaner, the first gas-powered airplane, the first Kellogg's Cornflakes, the first mass-produced crayons, the founding of the Boy Scouts, the development of the theory of relativity by Albert Einstein, sales of the first Model-T Ford, the first talking film by Thomas Edison, and the first hosting of the Olympic games by the United States. Telephones, too, were a relatively new invention, and automobiles were just starting to be driven. White gained local notoriety among his friends by being the first kid in his neighborhood to own a bicycle.

night was difficult "because it was the day he spent worrying about going back to school on Monday. School was consistently frightening, not so much in realization as in anticipation." This "boy" survived school by watching the black hands of the clock tick with teeth-gritting slowness toward the final bell. Then, he knew he could run home and return to the world that he loved best:

> This boy felt for animals a kinship he never felt for people. Against considerable opposition and with woefully inadequate equipment, he managed to provide himself with animals, so that he would never be without something to tend. . . . The total number of hours he spent just standing watching animals, or refilling their water pans, would be impossible to estimate; and it would be hard to say what he got out of it. . . . In spring he felt a sympathetic liberation with earth's renascence, and set a hen. He always seemed to be under some strange compulsion to assist the processes of incubation and germination, as though without him, they might fail and the earth grow old and die. To him a miracle was essentially egg-shaped.[3]

In August 1905, just after White celebrated his sixth birthday, his parents made their first family vacation to Great Pond, one of the Belgrade Lakes in Maine. This tradition continued for years and greatly influenced the rest of White's days.

The house they lived in was more than just charmingly "rustic." They had to creep out to an outhouse to use the toilet and trek to a nearby farmhouse to eat supper. "Roughing it" didn't bother White, who relished the humid evenings spent swinging in a hammock on the cabin's porch and the afternoons by the lake, many of

E.B. White at Great Pond, one of the Belgrade Lakes in Maine. His family began vacationing there when White was six years old and continued for many years. Though the house was rustic (they used an outhouse for a toilet), the house and area greatly influenced White. He was to spend most of his life alternating between life in bustling New York City and the rural Maine countryside.

which were spent in a sixteen-foot motorboat built by his brothers, Albert and Stanley. They named the boat *Jessie*, after their mother, who hated the water because she had never learned to swim. In the preface to *Letters of E.B. White*, he writes of those summer days:

> It was sheer enchantment. We Whites were city people—everything about Belgrade was a new experience: the freshwater lake, the pines and spruces and birches, the pasture with its sweet fern and juniper, the farmhouse where we took our meals, the rough camp with its sparsely furnished bedrooms, the backhouse with its can of chloride-of-lime, the boating, the swimming, and the company of other campers along the shore. The month of August was four solid weeks of heaven.
>
> The delicious smells and sounds of Belgrade are still with me after these many years of separation. I spent much of my time in a canoe, exploring bogs and streams, netting turtles. At night in bed, I fell asleep to the distant thump of a single-cylinder engine far out on the lake—a benign passage on dark waters. [On the canoe] Father would be in his round white flannel hat, Mother shading herself with a parasol, Lillian in ribbons and bows, Albert and Stanley nursing the brae little engine. . . . At Bean's store, Father would treat us to a round of Moxie or birch beer, and we could feed the bass that hung around the wharf and then head back across the lake, sometimes adding to the boat's already intolerable burden a case of Moxie—Father's favorite drink.[4]

There was another advantage to life at the lake. It temporarily relieved White of the hay fever that plagued him during the warm months of the year, causing his eyes to water and his nose to turn puffy and red from sneezing. His mother, following the advice of the family doctor, greeted each morning by pouring cold water onto White's head before breakfast. For the rest of his life, White battled the itchy, annoying demon of hay fever. It may have been his early wrestling with the nuisance of this illness that touched off a somewhat hypochondriac nature that continued to haunt him. But in August, he left the hay fever, his worries about school, and his general anxieties behind.

In his most often anthologized essay, "Once More to the Lake," published in August 1941, White describes going back to Maine with his ten-year-old son, Joel, and the strange feelings such a journey gave him. On one hand being at the lake brought back such powerful memories of his own childhood that he couldn't distinguish between his grown self and the boy he remembered. He'd look at his son and feel bewildered; seeing himself in his child, but also knowing his real and current role as a father. His emotions were spiked with bittersweet nostalgia, longing, and the understanding that he would never again be that boy he recalled so clearly:

It is strange how much you can remember about places like that once you allow your mind to return into the grooves that lead back. You remember one thing, and that suddenly reminds you of another thing. I guess I remembered clearest of all the early mornings, when the lake was cool and motionless, remembered how the bedroom smelled of the lumber it was made of and of the wet woods whose scent entered through the screen. The partitions in the camp were thin and did not extend clear to the top of the room, and I was always the first up I would dress softly so as not to wake the others, and sneak out into the sweet outdoors and start out in the canoe, keeping close along the shore in the long shadows of the pines. I remembered being very careful never to rub my paddle against the gunwale for fear of disturbing the stillness of the cathedral.[5]

E.B. White in 1920, at age twenty-one. By this time, White had graduated from Cornell University and was living at home, struggling to find his place in the world. He had many short-lived jobs in journalism, but found the writing to be boring and formulaic. He had more success and enjoyment writing more personal short pieces or poems that were often published by local newspapers.

2

A Thorough Education

WHITE DIDN'T KNOW how to talk to girls. When he was around them, his tongue seemed to swell to five times its normal size, his arms hung like weights at his sides, and all of the clever and interesting topics of conversation he had carefully rehearsed beforehand fled from his frantic mind. He explains these feelings of awkwardness:

In the matter of girls, I was different from most boys of my age. I admired girls a lot, but they terrified me. I did not feel that I possessed the peculiar gifts of accomplishments that girls liked in their male companions—the ability to dance, to play football, to cut up a bit in public, to smoke, and to make small talk. . . . In the four years I was in Mount Vernon High School, I never went to a school dance and I never took a girl to the drugstore for a soda or to the Westchester Playhouse or to Proctor's. I wanted to do these things but did not have the nerve.[6]

Eileen Thomas was a girl he managed to take to a dance at the Plaza Hotel in New York when he was a senior in high school. However, the date itself left him blushing with embarrassment at his social awkwardness. The formal dance required them to take the train for Grand Central and then the Fifth Avenue bus to the hotel. The trip there and back took almost as much time as the dance itself. Once at the Plaza, White, though his sister had tried to teach him to dance, maneuvered Eileen around the floor as though she were a mannequin, trying very hard not to count the steps out loud or step on her high heels. They rode back to Mount Vernon in near silence. White delivered Eileen to her front porch promptly at seven in the evening.

He did have a long-standing high school crush on Mildred Hesse, but only saw her at Siwanoy Pond, where the two of them would skate together on the ice, hardly speaking. He couldn't express to her in person how he felt. Instead, he wrote poems in which she was the central theme. White was learning that it was easier to express on paper what he'd never dream of saying in real life. Many years later, he does just this in remembering his time with Mildred Hesse:

Her eyes were blue and her ankles were strong. Together we must have covered hundreds of miles, sometimes leaving the pond proper and gliding into the woods on narrow fingers of ice. We didn't talk much, never embraced, we just skated for the ecstasy of skating—a magical glide. After one of these sessions, I would go home and play *Liebestraum* on the [piano], bathed in the splendor of perfect love and natural fatigue. This brief interlude on the ice, in the days of my youth, had a dreamlike quality, a purity, that has stayed with me all my life; and when nowadays I see a winter sky and feel the wind dropping with the sun and the naked trees against a reddening west, I remember what it was like to be in love before any of love's complexities or realities or disturbances had entered in, to dilute its splendor and challenge its perfection.[7]

In his last year at Mount Vernon High, White became the assistant editor of the school literary magazine, *The Oracle*. While he was there, he wrote two stories, an editorial that urged America to stay out of World War I, and his own version of Henry Wadsworth Longfellow's poem *Hiawatha*. He also sent a letter of protest to a magazine called *The American Boy*, urging hunters to quit cruelly trapping fur-bearing animals to earn money.

In the fall of 1917, White kept his promise to himself to follow in his brother's footsteps and attend Cornell University in upstate New York. Because of his good work in school, he set off to college with $1,000 worth of scholarships. White was so taken by his first experience on his own that he missed registration day for classes, instead spending the first few days exploring downtown Ithaca.

At that time, the United States was just entering into World War I. White was aware of the war, but not sure how he felt about it. On one hand, he realized that the United States could not remain neutral. On the other hand, he hated the idea of people being killed. He went back and forth between being concerned about the war and being distracted by the pressures of his daily life, which at times seemed very far away from the conflict occurring overseas.

In an essay written in October of 1939 as World War II was beginning, White reflected on his thoughts from so many years before. He reread the journal he kept in 1917, noting that he spent as much time worrying about an upcoming canoe trip as he did about the war:

> May 14, 1917. Yesterday I heard Billy Sunday deliver his booze sermon.

> May 27, 1917. I don't know what to do this summer. The country is at war and I think I ought to serve. Strange that the greatest war in history of the world is now going on, and it is hard to get men to enlist.

> June 3, 1917. I'm feeling extraordinarily patriotic tonight after having read the papers. . . . The struggle in Europe isn't over by any means, and so much history is being made every minute that it's up to every last one of us to see that it's the right kind

Did you know...

Cornell University has a long history of prestigious alumni. Along with E.B. White, other famous Cornell graduates include: Dr. Joyce Brothers, author, psychologist, and television personality; Pearl S. Buck, Pulitzer Prize winner and author of *The Good Earth*; Ruth Bader Ginsburg, United States Supreme Court justice; Lee Teng-hui, President of the Republic of China; Ed Lu, NASA astronaut; Toni Morrison, author and Nobel laureate; Thomas Pynchon, author; the late Christopher Reeve, actor; Kurt Vonnegut, author of *Slaughterhouse-Five* and *Breakfast of Champions*.

of history. It is my firm conviction that only the unstinted giving of time, money, and resources of the American people can save this world from its most terrible doom.

June 7, 1917. I guess there is no place in the world for me. I've been trying to get a job since Monday, and have failed. Yesterday afternoon I applied at G—'s School of Popular Music for a job playing piano at a summer hotel in the Catskills.[8]

White joined the Student Army Training Corps in July 1917, the summer before his sophomore year of college, and on September 12, he registered for the draft. Before he could be called to duty, World War I ended at 2:15 A.M. on November 11, 1918.

Despite the surrounding political turmoil, White enjoyed his days as a college student at Cornell. One of the best things that happened to him at Cornell was that he earned the nickname "Andy" from his friends, after the first president of the University, Andrew D. White. It was a tradition at Cornell to give anyone with the last name "White" the new title of "Andy." White, who had always felt embarrassed by the strange name of "Elwyn," was very happy to have a new way of being addressed. He joined Phi Gamma Delta and eventually was elected president of the fraternity. He started writing for the *Cornell Daily Sun*, a daily local newspaper that almost everyone in town read religiously. Because of his writing and editing talents, he was elected editor-in-chief in the spring semester of 1920.

An important part of his life at that time was his membership in an informal group of faculty and students known as the Manuscript Club. The group met on Saturday nights in the library of English literature professor Martin Sampson's home to talk about writing, and, most importantly, share their work. All members (which consisted of several faculty and students) were required to bring a piece of writing. It could be anything they'd written: a poem, a short story, or an essay. The writings were then collected and put in a cardboard box. None of the writers signed their work. After that, the manuscripts were pulled out at random and read aloud to the group. The group would then discuss the work; what they liked, what wasn't working, and so on. Because no one knew the author's identity, the comments and suggestions were more honest and the writer's ego was protected.

During his junior year, White took an advanced writing course, English 8, with Professor William Strunk, Jr. From the beginning, White admired Strunk, who he described as friendly, funny, and absolutely adamant about what constituted good writing. Strunk taught class using *The Elements of Style*, a forty-three-page manuscript he wrote that contained what he saw as the necessary fundamentals of writing. White could not have known then that thirty-seven years later, Macmillan Publishing Company would ask him to revise the book for mass publication. The text remains a standard of college English classes today. White wrote the introduction for the book. In it, he fondly recalls Strunk's teaching method:

> "Omit needless words!" cries the author on page 23, and into that imperative Will Strunk really put his heart and soul. In the days when I was sitting in his class, he omitted so many needless words, and omitted them so forcibly and with such eagerness and obvious relish, that he often seemed in the position of having shortchanged himself. . . . Will Strunk got out of this predicament by a simple trick: he uttered every sentence three times. When he delivered his oration on brevity to the class, he leaned forward over his desk, grasping his coat lapels in his hands, and, in a husky, conspiratorial voice said, "Rule Seventeen. Omit needless words! Omit needless words! Omit needless words!"[9]

In his last year at Cornell, White happened to attend *Aria da Capo*, a play written by Edna St. Vincent Millay. His eyes fastened on the pretty girl playing the part of Columbine. Alice Burchfield, or "Burch" as her friends called her, was a smart and popular junior student from Buffalo, New York. White immediately began escorting her to movies, ballgames, and long walks along Six-Mile Creek. Finally, he had met a girl who he didn't have to adore from afar, one who he could actually talk to without falling over in fright. Alice's lively, friendly manner and sparkling blue eyes allowed White to relax, and he wrote poems to her, which he published in the *Sun* under the pseudonym of "D'Annunzio." In "O Oculi," White jokingly writes of how he thought the most wonderful eyes of all were from his dog, until he met someone (Alice) who startled him into realizing that a human being could have eyes of greater interest. "The gol darn orbs are bottomless;/ And must observe from sense of duty/Their depth surpasses not their beauty."[10] Luckily, Alice had a good sense of humor and was pleased rather than offended by his comparing her eyes with a dog's. White graduated from Cornell in June 1921, but for the next two years he would continue to maintain a relationship with Alice, one that fluctuated between marriage-bound love and affectionate friendship, depending on his mood or state of mind. In fact, much of their relationship after he graduated was managed through letters and the occasional visit. For the most part, after White said good-bye to the rolling green hills of Cornell's campus, he never again was as committed to Alice as he had been sitting with her in the athletic field bleachers, holding hands, and searching the sky for falling stars.

Upon graduation, White had received his diploma, slaps of congratulations from his Phi Gamma Delta brothers, and a job offer from Professor Sampson to be an English instructor at the University of Minnesota. (White refused. He still shuddered at the thought of standing in front of a group of people.) Yet White felt the anxiety of not knowing how to become part of the "real" grown-up world he had been afraid to face even as a child. How was it that everyone else seemed to know who they were and what they wanted to do, whereas he felt as though he were constantly struggling to find his place in the world?

White returned home to Mount Vernon and began looking for a job in Manhattan. The country was in the middle of the depression, and jobs were hard to come by. He put an ad in the "Positions Wanted" section of *Editor and Publisher* magazine and, within a week, had a job offer with the United Press, located in the Pulitzer Building in New York City. The United Press sent out daily reports at a near constant pace, and because their goal was to be the first to announce a particular story, White was of the opinion that they often sacrificed accuracy for speed. He wrote two wickedly biting poems on the evils of bad journalism before quitting a week later, disgusted with the sensationalism and exploitation he saw as the newsperson's job: Get the most outrageous story, use human tragedy to sell papers, and don't worry whose privacy you invade in the meantime. White bumped from one job to the next, until he secured a position with the American Legion News Service, where he wrote press releases for their publicity department. The writing itself was boring and formulaic, so White continued to write his own pieces in his journal, or poems that were often published by local newspapers. Each day started to feel like the one before it. He wasn't challenged in his job, he missed his friends, and he still had no idea what he was meant to do with his life. So when a buddy from Cornell, Howard "Cush"

Cushman, suggested that the two of them set out on an American adventure across the country, White hesitated for about as long as it took to say "yes."

On March 9, 1922, the two friends set out in White's brand new Model-T Ford roadster he christened "Hotspur," ready to face life on the open road. They equipped themselves with camping gear, two Corona typewriters, $400, clothes, notebook paper and pens, a hunting knife, warm sweaters and socks, cooking equipment, and a mouth organ. In those days, cross-country traveling was an unusual decision. Cars had only been in use for a short time, road maps were vague, and there were long stretches of unmarked land. This was part of what attracted White to the idea in the first place; he could escape into the "wilderness" of America while heading west and write about it along the way.

For the next six months, the two friends traveled from upstate New York all the way to Seattle, in search of the adventures that awaited them on the wide open roads of America. White and his friend, Cush, would, indeed, experience adventure, although maybe not the kind they had envisioned when they hatched the great idea of hitting the open road. No, their "adventures" (if you could call them that) stemmed from their constant lack of money and the unreliability of Hotspur. For example, Hotspur would get temperamental and overheat. On at least one occasion, White dislocated his right elbow and had to change gears on Hotspur one-handed (Cush, having never learned to drive, was of no help). Throughout the trip, White held several odd jobs: working for a day at an ad agency signing the name "Horace C. Klein" to letter after letter, playing foxtrots on the piano at a local café, sand-papering a dance floor, washing dishes, and running a concession stand at a carnival in Cody, Wyoming. He also made money by

E.B. White next to his car, nicknamed "Hotspur," during a cross-country adventure with his friend Howard "Cush" Cushman. White had dislocated his right elbow during the trip and is shown here with his arm in a makeshift sling. With characteristic humor, he noted across from the photograph, "We are in Walker, Minnesota. . . . Sweet are the uses of suitcase straps."

jotting down poems, limericks, or stories and submitting them to places like the *Minneapolis Journal*, the *Minneapolis Sunday Tribune*, and *The Ladies Home Journal*.

In one particular instance in Kentucky, the two lost money betting on Auntie May instead of the winning horse in the 1922 Kentucky Derby. White recovered from the loss by writing a sonnet of praise to the winner, Morvich, a poem the *Louisville Herald* subsequently published on the front page of the paper after paying White $5.

When the pair reached Seattle, Washington, Cushman decided he'd had enough and White decided he'd stay for a while. He found a $40-a-week job as a reporter and then as a columnist at the *Seattle Times*. Not surprisingly, White eventually found that he and the job were incompatible. "I discovered that I would never make a good newspaper reporter," he once explained. "It was out of the question. The city editor discovered it; he knew even before I did. I was not quick enough or alert enough—I was always taking the wrong train going in the wrong direction."[11]

One day, White impulsively bought a first-class ticket on the *S.S. Buford*, a ship headed on a forty-day cruise that would take him through the Bering Strait to Siberia, Alaska, and then back to Washington. For the first half of the journey, White enjoyed the privileges of first-class, dancing and dining with the rest of the well-off seagoers. Then, once they reached Skagway, he found his pockets empty. Ever resourceful, he succeeded in convincing the captain to give him a job as a saloon-boy, surprising the passengers he had lounged with early on by waiting on them that same evening. He continued working as a member of the crew for the duration of the journey, later moving below deck to work as firemen's messboy after the previous messboy had been knifed. When the ship returned to the West Coast, White, heeding his father's advice, bought a railroad ticket and headed back east.

White was twenty-four, living at home with his parents, and still unclear about his future. At the time, he viewed himself a failure. In truth, his experiences as editor and writer in high school and college, his observations on his travels across the United States, his work with daily deadlines on the *Seattle Times*, and his continued journal entries about life on the *S.S. Buford* all contributed to shaping the famous writer he would soon become.

*E.B. White and his wife Katherine shown at work during their days at **The New Yorker**. White met Katherine when she was a fiction editor at the magazine and White was working there on a part-time basis. This was an arrangement that was to last for most of their lives together. They began working at **The New Yorker** when it was a young magazine, and they were to contribute greatly to its development and success.*

3

Manhattan and *The New Yorker*: City Mouse

STARTING IN THE fall of 1923, White spent two years commuting into New York City to work as a layout person for Frank Seaman and Company advertising agency on Park Avenue in Manhattan. His job required none of his writing skills, but White fulfilled that need for himself by continuing to write in his journal and composing poems that were published in places like the *New York Evening Post* and the *New York World*.

By the summer of 1925, White's tolerance for the commute and the job itself had worn out. He and three fellow fraternity brothers from Cornell rented an apartment at 112 West Thirteenth Street in Greenwich Village. Once again, White wasn't sure what to do with himself. While his housemates all had jobs, he describes his perspective on the suddenly silent moments after his friends scrambled out of the house on their way to work:

> Those mornings alone in the apartment straightening up after the others had left for work, rinsing the dirty cereal-encrusted bowls, taking the percolator apart and putting it together again, and then sinking down on the lumpy old couch in the terrible loneliness of midmorning, some-times giving way to tears of doubt and misgiving. . . . and in the back room the compensatory window box with the brave and grimy seedlings struggling, and the view of the naked fat lady across the yard. It had always been a question then of how to get through the day, the innumerable aimless journeys to remote sections of the town, inspecting warehouses, docks, marshes, lumber-yards, the interminable quest for the holy and unnamable grail, looking for it down every street and in every window and in every pair of eyes, following a star always obscured by mists.[12]

Like most things, White's experience of Manhattan was mixed. He classified it as a place that will "bestow the gift of loneliness and the gift of privacy. . . . It can destroy the individual or it can fulfill him, depending a good deal on luck. No one should come to New York to live unless he is willing to be lucky." He appreciated the fact that the city had been where many famous writers, including Walt Whitman, Willa Cather, and Ernest Hemingway, first came to see if they could "make it" as writers. He also was aware of how alive the city was at every second of the day, how something was always happening, maybe in the apartment next door, down the street by the seaport, in the air above. White believed that there were three types of New Yorkers: those who were born there, those who commuted into the city every day, and those who were born somewhere else and rushed to New York in search of something greater. He was, of course, of the third type, and maybe that is why he was able to see:

> New York's high-strung disposition, its poetical deportment, its dedication to the arts, and its incomparable achievements. Commuters give the city its tidal restlessness, natives give it solidity and continuity, but the settlers give it passion. And whether it is a farmer arriving from Italy to set up a small grocery store in a slum, or a young girl arriving from a small town in Mississippi to escape the indignity of being observed by her neighbors, or a boy arriving from the Corn Belt with a manuscript in his suitcase and a pain in his heart, it makes no difference, each embraces New York with the intense excitement of first love, each absorbs New York with the fresh eyes of an adventurer, each generates heat and light to dwarf the Consolidated Edison Company.[13]

The New Yorker was a new magazine meant to differ significantly from its contemporaries; a weekly publication that offered profiles, interviews, essays on topical concerns, poetry, short fiction, and movie, book, and art reviews. White picked up an issue for fifteen cents on Saturday, February 21, 1925, three days after the magazine had been released to the public for the first time. He liked it immediately; he liked that it was clever, liberal, and different from the conventional and conservative magazines being published. The pieces were in a short and witty style of writing that White felt confident he could duplicate. He jotted down a short piece about springtime and sent it to the address listed under "submission guidelines." Almost right away, he received a reply that *The New Yorker* would publish the piece. He submitted another and then another piece, mostly short sketches of observations he made while roaming the zoo or docks or small restaurants of New York. He managed to capture the difficulty of the human experience in a humorous way. In "Child's Play," he related an incident of a waitress in a bustling coffee shop who accidentally spilled buttermilk on White's jacket. He recounts his

Did you know...

The New Yorker is still published every week to a wide circulation of readers. The "Notes and Comments" and "The Talk of the Town," as well as the short newsbreaks White wrote, continue to be features of the magazine. Several books have been written about *The New Yorker*, including James Thurber's *The Years with Ross*; Dale Kramer's *Ross and The New Yorker*; Thomas Kunkel's *Genius in Disguise: Harold Ross of The New Yorker*; Renata Adler's *Gone: The Last Days of The New Yorker*; Gigi Mahon's *The Last Days of The New Yorker*; and Mary Corey's *The World Through a Monocle*. E.B. White is featured in each as a major shaper of the magazine's sustained success.

embarrassment and his slapstick reaction, as well as his attempts to make the very upset waitress feel better. The story had a tone of self-mocking and wit, and readers responded favorably to it. It wasn't long before Katharine Sergeant Angell, the literary editor at the magazine, suggested to her boss, Harold Ross, that they hire this witty and insightful writer.

Katharine Sergeant Angell was an unconventional woman for her day. She worked long hours at the magazine, offering her intelligent editorial skills and advice, while at the same time raising two children, Nancy and Roger. A graduate of the women's college Bryn Mawr, Katharine was initially hired in the summer of 1925 to work part-time as a reader. It soon became apparent to Harold Ross that the magazine needed and would greatly benefit from her being in the office full-time as Ross's editorial assistant. She accepted. At the time White met Katharine, she was near the end of an unhappy relationship to Ernest Angell, a former Army man and lawyer, who she married when she was much younger. From the beginning, White recalls being struck by her competence, lightning-sharp editorial abilities, commanding demeanor, and dark hair and startling blue eyes.

However, when White was offered a full-time job at *The New Yorker*, he declined. As always, he was reluctant to be stuck in an office or in a situation that wouldn't allow him a significant amount of personal time. In January 1927, he agreed to part-time employment, under the stipulation that he be allowed to come and go as he pleased, provided that he met his deadlines. Ross liked White's work so much that he agreed. He gave White an office to share with writer James Thurber, who became one of White's closest lifelong friends. When the two were

Humorist James Thurber in 1934. Thurber and E.B. White became good friends when they shared an office at The New Yorker. *Thurber's comic drawings of cats, dogs, and people became a regular part of the magazine, much like White's contributions were. Thurber once said, "No one can write a sentence like White."*

in the office together, White noticed Thurber penning quick and funny doodles, which he subsequently threw into the trash. White fished out the crumpled-up pieces of paper and showed the sketches to Ross. From then on, Thurber's comic drawings of people, cats and dogs, and city life became a regular part of the magazine.

White's work at *The New Yorker* consisted of him writing funny little pieces known as newsbreaks, captions for cartoons, a "Notes and Comments" column, and "Talk of the Town" articles. The "Notes and Comments" pieces were parodies of the typical editorial. White used this form to poke fun at everything from book clubs to President Calvin Coolidge to the solo flight of Charles Lindbergh in 1927. Harper Brothers published *The Lady is Cold*, a slender volume of his poetry, on May 1, 1929. The book met with rave reviews. Amid his writing, White managed to travel to Europe, to work as a summer counselor at Camp Otter in Ontario, Canada, and, perhaps most importantly, to find himself falling in love with the dynamic Katharine Angell.

White knew that Katharine's marriage was coming to an end on its own, and he also became aware that she reciprocated his feelings of love. The two were cautious though about how to proceed. Both worried about the reaction and well being of Katharine's two children, aged eleven and eight at the time. Ultimately, Katharine and Ernest divorced, an action largely unheard of in the 1920s. Ernest had primary custody of Nancy and Roger, which was also unusual for the time period. Still, Katharine thought it best to be as amicable as possible in the divorce and agreed not to fight her husband on the custody battle. She would content herself with the arrangement, even though it meant that her children would live with her on weekends and holidays only.

Shortly thereafter, on a bright Wednesday morning, November 13, 1929, White and Katharine impulsively hopped into his car, along with Katharine's little Scottish Terrier, Daisy, and sped fifty miles to the countryside of Bedford Village, where they were married in a Presbyterian church. They didn't tell their family or friends beforehand; others only learned about it when the two returned to work the very next day. White, in typical fashion, expressed his joy at their marriage in writing, sending Katharine an interoffice memo. It was a copy of a *New Yorker* cartoon of a man sitting on a curb, lost in thought. Underneath it, White wrote "E.B. White slowly accustomed himself to the idea that he had made the most beautiful decision of his life." [14]

After their marriage, White moved into Katharine's apartment on 16 East Eighth Street in New York. In the summer of 1930, Katharine told White that she was pregnant. Again, she worried that her two children from her first marriage would be upset, but on the contrary, both were excited about the idea of having a new baby brother or sister. As far as White was concerned, Katharine's pregnancy was a cause for celebration and he looked forward to the day he would be a father with a sense of excitement, apprehension, and awe. Joel McCoun White came into the world on December 21, 1930, by caesarean section in Harbor Hospital. Because a caesarean section was a fairly new and dangerous procedure then, Katharine and Joel were still in the hospital on New Year's Eve. White wrote a letter to his new son, welcoming him into the world and family through the persona of the family dog, "Daisy":

The tree that holds your star will be shedding its needles very soon—they will drop like rain, and the electric lights in the colored bulbs will be turned out, but I have noticed that new things always spring up somewhat methodically and for every darkened Christmas tree ornament there is a white flower in spring. Or, in this particular apartment, even before spring. There are some here now called Narcissus, so come home and see them Joel, and wishing you a very Happy New Year I am. . . . Faithfully yrs, Daisy.[15]

WALDEN;

OR,

LIFE IN THE WOODS.

By HENRY D. THOREAU,

AUTHOR OF "A WEEK ON THE CONCORD AND MERRIMACK RIVERS."

I do not propose to write an ode to dejection, but to brag as lustily as chanticleer in the morning, standing on his roost, if only to wake my neighbors up. — Page 92.

BOSTON:

TICKNOR AND FIELDS.

M DCCC LIV.

Henry David Thoreau, writer of E.B. White's favorite book, *Walden,* published initially in 1854. For a two-year period, Thoreau lived in a small cabin in the woods and wrote of his experience with only the land and animals to keep him company. He wrote: "I went to the woods because I wished to live deliberately, to front only the essential facts of life, and see if I could not learn what it had to teach, and not, when I came to die, discover that I had not lived." Periodically, White felt the same need to leave modern society and retreat to a solitary rural life.

4

The Writing Life

THERE WAS ONLY one book that White carried with him everywhere—from his travels across country, his Alaskan adventures, and his frequent moves between Manhattan and Maine. That book was Henry David Thoreau's *Walden*. In *Walden*, Thoreau writes about the contentment and happiness obtained through simplicity in life, mainly as it is found in the peacefulness of the countryside. Thoreau describes his decision in 1845 to escape the clamor of the social world by moving into the woods and building his own house. *Walden* is more or less a journal of Thoreau's thoughts and activities while living alone day to day with only the land and its animal inhabitants to keep him company. To his readers, Thoreau recommended this return to the simple life unburdened by materialism, taking strength from nature and stopping to observe the slow ballet of falling leaves or the music of the wind sighing through the trees at nightfall. White related completely to this way of life. He, too, wanted the luxury to think and write without the distractions of modern life intruding. Luckily, Katharine understood White's relatively solitary nature and did not object when he needed to slip off by himself.

In the fall months of 1933, Katharine and White found the perfect summer get-away, a rustic farmhouse located in North Brooklin, Maine. It was a twelve-room home with a barn, boathouse, and forty acres of land. Though the family spent summers there, which allowed White time away from his work at *The New Yorker*, White started to feel caged in by the constant dead-lines of the magazine. In 1935, his father died, and nine months later, he lost his mother to cancer. In the same year, a close friend also died, and Katharine suffered a miscarriage. Perhaps these tragic events, along with White's increased physical ailments, caused him to reconsider his life. He was in his mid-thirties, and, though he had published extensively, White didn't feel himself to be a successful writer. On August 7, 1937, White wrote his good-bye article to *The New Yorker*, announcing to readers, his friends, and his family that he wanted to take a year off to focus on writing a book.

While Katharine and Joel remained in New York, White lived in the farmhouse in Maine, focusing his energy into completing a long poem called "Zoo Revisited: Or the

Life and Death of Ollie Hackstaff." Strangely though, White found that he couldn't throw himself into the poem as he could other projects. Try as he might, his days started to contain less and less disciplined writing time and more frequent walks to admire the countryside. By January 1938, White wrote of his confusion to James Thurber. "I have made an unholy mess of this 'year off' business. I haven't produced two cents worth of work, have broken my wife's health, my own spirit, and two or three lampshades by getting my feet tangled in the cord." To which Thurber replied, "You may be a writer in farmer's clothing but you are still a writer." Thurber was right. In April 1938, White gave up. His year off had lasted only nine months.

However, being in the country for an extended amount of time confirmed for White that he didn't want to continue to live in the chaotic world of the city. He begged Katharine to do her editorial work for *The New Yorker* from their house in Maine. He argued that it would be better for Joel, now seven years old, to have the kind of childhood White had benefited from—skating on the pond in the winter, taking the boat out onto the lake in the summer, hiking, and being able to do these things year-round instead of during stolen weekends here and there. Katharine agreed and in the spring of 1938, the family set up a permanent home at the farmhouse in North Brooklin, where they remained for the next five years. While White still wrote the occasional piece for *The New Yorker*, his main source of income was a monthly column for *Harper's Magazine* called "One Man's Meat."

White immediately began setting up the farmer's life on the forty acres they owned. He filled the barn and yard with chickens, geese, roosters, sheep, dogs, and a pig. White realized his animal population was a bit excessive:

> I have fifteen sheep; also own one-half of a full-blooded Oxford Down ram with another fellow. Two of the sheep are dungy tails; two are snotty noses, one is black. In general their health is good, no ticks. The ram is gentle. I have 112 New Hampshire Rode pullets in the henhouse and 36 White Plymouth Rock pullets in the barn, a total of 148 layers, I have three Toulouse geese, the remnants of a flock of four, one having been taken by a fox. I have six roosters, celibates, living to themselves. There is also a dog, a tomcat, a pig, and a captive mouse.[16]

Though being outside made his hay fever worse, he thrived on the routine of rising in the morning to feed the animals, check on the chicken's eggs, and take care of the garden with Katharine. The quiet life allowed him to read

Did you know...

For many years, E.B. White carried around a dog-eared copy of Henry David Thoreau's *Walden*. He liked Thoreau's ideas about living a simple life. White wrote several essays about the man and the book. In one essay, "Walden," White directly compares his move from Manhattan to Maine to Thoreau's solitary life at Walden. He also identified heavily with one of Thoreau's most popular quotes that many humans lead lives of "quiet desperation."

much more, often spending time after dinner by the fireplace with Joel, reading novels out loud. He liked the feel of small community life and felt relieved to be able to send Joel to a small two-room schoolhouse that was quite unlike the large public school his son had attended in New York. In a letter to his brother, Stanley, White expressed his love of the place:

> Our woodlot is full of hemlock, spruce, birch, juniper, and all the aromatic sweetness of a Maine pasture; yet it dips right down to the tidewaters, where gulls scream their heads off and hair-seals bark like old love-sick terriers. . . . Many days are startlingly clear and blue, many are thick a-fog. The fog shuts in fast, catching you short when you are sailing. . . . Off the coast are hundreds and hundreds of outlying islands, some tiny, some very big. . . . The prevailing winds are from the south-west, and they make up strong in the afternoon and blow smokey.[17]

He finally found himself modeling the simple life in the country, as his hero Thoreau did.

Still, White did not lose himself so completely in the farm work that he neglected his writing. In October 1938, he published a collection of poems called *The Fox and the Peacock* and in March 1939 *Quo Vadimus? Or the Case for the Bicycle* appeared in bookstores. *Quo Vadimus?* was a compilation of humorous essays. Book critics from well-known places like *The New York Times*, *Time*, and *The New York Tribune* reviewed it favorably, and he realized he was starting to earn the reputation of a talented essayist and humorist. He and Katharine published an 800-page anthology of collected humor pieces from writers such as Benjamin Franklin, Washington Irving, Mark Twain, and

Ring Larder called *A Subtreasury of American Humor* in November 1941. This book too met with critical acclaim. For White, humor spoke to the universal human experience; to him, the ability to laugh and see what's funny in a given situation remained as essential as breathing:

> One of the things commonly said about humorists is that they are really very sad people—clowns with a breaking heart. There is some truth in it, but it is badly stated. It would be more accurate, I think, to say that there is a deep vein of melancholy running through everyone's life and that a humorist, perhaps more sensible of it than some others, compensates for it actively and positively. . . . As everyone knows, there is often a rather fine line between laughing and crying, and if a humorous piece of writing brings a person to the point where his emotional responses are untrustworthy and seem likely to break over into the opposite realm, it is because humorous writing, like poetical writing, has an extra content. It plays, like an active child, close to the big hot fire which is Truth. And sometimes the reader feels the heat.[18]

White continued writing for *Harper's Magazine*. His monthly pieces were so well liked that White published another book in June 1942 simply called *One Man's Meat*, a compilation of the articles he'd written for the magazine. Again, his book met with great critical praise, and the first edition sold around 12,000 copies.

As he had ever since he was first published, he wrote not only about his observations of daily life, but also about political topics, one of which became the growing conflict in Europe, and Hitler's frightening rise to power. Using his own experience of how his family reacted to the announcement that England had declared war on Germany on September 3, 1939, White gave readers a window through which to view the war's impact. White saw Hitler's actions as not something far away and intangible, but a real threat to personal and national freedom. When the United States became involved in 1941, White anticipated that the war would have devastating and long-lasting consequences. He started to doubt the value of remaining in Maine. In the preface of *One Man's Meat,* he tried to put into words the conflict he felt about his life in the country during the war and how the essays related to it:

> It is a collection of essays which I wrote from a salt water farm in Maine while engaged in trivial, peaceful pursuits, knowing all the time that the world hadn't arranged any true peace or granted anyone the privilege of indulging himself for long in trivialities. Although such a record is likely to seem incongruous, I see no harm in preserving it, the more so since I have begun to receive letters from soldiers overseas assuring me that there is a positive value to them in the memory of peace and home.[19]

Harold Ross, the editor of *The New Yorker,* told White that the magazine had lost several good writers to the armed forces. He worried that the magazine would have to shift from appearing once a week to every other week. After hearing this news, White and Katharine decided that they could contribute more to the war effort if they moved back to the city, where they could join the staff of *The New Yorker* in making the public aware of what was happening overseas. White hoped that through his editorials published in the magazine he could help end the war as well as write about his plan for world peace through the establishment of a universal and united government system. Though he was

The front page of The New York Times *from December 12, 1941, only five days after United States battleships had been attacked at Pearl Harbor. In 1944, E.B. White and his wife Katherine left their rural life in Maine to return to New York City and contribute to the war effort by writing about the U.S. involvement overseas. White's increased involvement with* The New Yorker *led to his increased visibility as a writer of national prominence.*

able to address such topics in *Harper's Magazine*, it was published only once a month, whereas *The New Yorker* hit the newsstands every week. In 1944, White once again gave up his country life to return with Katharine to an apartment in Greenwich Village on West Eleventh Street in the heart of Manhattan. Happily, the city streets did not depress White, as he had feared they might, but reinvigorated him.

For the next several years, White and his family would remain in New York City, returning to Maine only for short vacations in the summer. Though White missed his menagerie of animals, the lake, and the barn, he felt called to a higher purpose. Through his editorials he hoped to persuade the American people that great steps were needed to end the war and to establish a way to present future conflicts from occurring. He collected such a large number of essays on the topic of a world government that the fall of 1946 saw the publication of a collection of writings titled *The Wild Flag*.

In recognition of his merits as a writer and thinker, White earned great praise during 1945 and 1946. He won the Limited Editions Club's Gold Medal for *One Man's Meat*, the Newspaper Guild's award went to *The New Yorker* in large part because of his contributions, and White was offered membership in the National Institute of Arts and Letters.

Truly, in a short span of time, White had made good on his promise to himself and his family to become a well-known writer. Though his parents had not survived to see him make it into the national consciousness, White felt some relief in having established himself. Despite the fact that he no longer lived his life as Thoreau recommended, White believed he was right where he wanted and needed to be.

The late television host Johnny Carson shakes hands with the star of Stuart Little, *a television movie about a mouse with the same name. Carson was the off-camera narrator for the television special based on E.B. White's book. White published* Stuart Little *in 1945, after composing the book from many short tales he had written over many years.*

5

Of Mice and Men

EVEN AS AN adult, White retained the ability to see the world with the eyes of a child. He found himself constantly amazed, particularly by the beauty of nature and the simple things it produced, like the perfect oval of a freshly laid egg. He believed that children understood and observed the world in a more natural and real way than adults did. He also had strong memories of his childhood summers in Wilson's Woods, winter skating across the frozen Siwanoy Pond, and annual family trips to the rented camp on Great Pond.

One of the strong remembrances he had involved a mouse. "Once, when I was a child, sick in bed, I had a mouse take up with me. He was a common house mouse and I think must have been a young one, as he was friendly and without fear. I made a home for him, complete with a gymnasium, and he learned many fine tricks and was pleasant company."[20] The little mouse appeared again to him on a train ride to New York in the 1920s, when he feel asleep and dreamed of "a small little character who had the features of a mouse, was nicely dressed, courageous, and questing."[21] When he woke up, White jotted down a few notes about the mouse. He named the mouse Stuart and began to write short episodes about him to tell to his young nephews and nieces. Soon, he had a desk drawer full of Stuart Little tales. In a letter to his friend Eugene Saxton in March 1939, White wrote this about the hero of his first children's book:

> You will be shocked and grieved to discover that the principal character in the story has somewhat the attributes and appearance of a mouse. This does not mean that I am either challenging or denying Mr. Disney's genius. At the risk of seeming a very whimsical fellow indeed, I will have to break down and confess to you that Stuart Little appeared to me in a dream, all complete, with his hat, his cane, and his brisk manner. Since he was the only fictional figure ever to honor and disturb my sleep, I was deeply touched, and felt that I was not free to change him into a grasshopper or a wallaby. Luckily, he bears no resemblance, either physically or temperamental, to Mickey [Mouse]. I guess that's a break for all of us.[22]

However, White's true inspiration for composing the children's book *Stuart Little* at the age of forty-five sprung not from the same whimsy the book weaves, but rather from a dark cloud of depression he endured on and off throughout his life. Though he had been writing and publishing for decades, he still wasn't convinced he had accomplished anything worthwhile. He also harbored deep fears of dying suddenly; a fear perhaps brought on by his constant struggle with hay fever and other physical ailments. White put together his scattered tales of Stuart in just eight short weeks, and *Stuart Little* was published by Harper & Brothers in October 1945.

The book tells of the adventures of an uncanny character, two inches high, named Stuart, who is the second son of Mr. and Mrs. Frederick C. Little and a younger brother to George Little. A neat chap with his jaunty hat, blue worsted suit, and small cane, Stuart is not your typical child. "The truth of the matter was, the baby looked very much like a mouse in every way. He was only about two inches high; and he had a mouse's sharp nose, a mouse's tail, a mouse's whiskers, and the pleasant, shy nature of a mouse" (*Stuart Little* 1–2). The Little family must adjust to Stuart's small size. They make him a bed from a cigarette box with four clothespins supporting it and give him ice skates constructed from paper clips. Together, the family lives happily in a pretty house in New York City.

Stuart's small size makes him useful for many unusual chores. He fetches his mother's wedding ring when it tumbles down the bathroom drain, fixes the sticky keys on the family piano, and retrieves lost ping-pong balls from under radiators. In turn, the Littles accommodated the house to suit Stuart's needs. He turns on the bathroom light by pulling on a long string that reaches to the floor and has a special collection of doll-sized things to use to keep himself tidy—a miniature toothbrush, soap, washcloth, and comb for his whiskers.

White's Stuart is much like the author himself. Stuart is a well-groomed individual who lives in New York and has a thirst for adventure and the open road. Like White, Stuart loves the water and sailing. In one chapter, he sails along the pond in Central Park and signs up for a job working on the *Wasp*, a black schooner with a three-inch canon and a sturdy sail. Next, he participates in a race with the *Lillian B. Womrath*, a fierce boat owned by a "fat, sulky boy of twelve, named LeRoy. He wore a blue serge suit and a white necktie stained with orange juice" (*Stuart Little* 37). By braving a storm and a collision, and by never giving up, Stuart crosses the finish line first. The novel doesn't ignore White's romantic nature either. Stuart meets a brown hen-bird with a streak of yellow named Margalo. He is so enamored with her that he runs away from home to find her when she flees. Stuart sets off in a six-inch-long yellow model car that can turn invisible; a dream car not unlike the Model-T Ford White drove across country after college. In some cases, White makes Stuart braver than himself. Unlike White, who feared public speaking, Stuart has no

Did you know...

The tiny Stuart Little keeps famous company with other miniature characters in children's literature such as Tom Thumb, Thumbelina, the Borrowers, and Jonathan Swift's Lilliputians in *Gulliver's Travels*. White's *Stuart Little* has been compared to *The Wind in the Willows* and Lewis Carrol's *Alice in Wonderland* because of its skillful blending of the wondrous with the real.

problem being a substitute for School Number Seven when the teacher, Miss Gunderson, takes ill. Dressed in a salt-and-pepper jacket, striped pants, a tie, and small glasses, Stuart authoritatively teaches his pupils. During class, one of the students echoes a long-held sentiment of White's, that it's not money or fame or an accumulation of things that are important in life, but simple things like "a shaft of sunlight at the end of a dark afternoon, a note in music, and the way the back of a baby's neck smells if its mother keeps it tidy" (*Stuart Little* 92).

In the last chapter, Stuart has still not found Margalo, but neither has he given up the search. After a failed date with the two-inch high Harriet Ames, Stuart "rose from the ditch, climbed into his car, and started up the road that led toward the north. The sun was just coming up over the hills on his right. As he peered ahead into the great land that stretched before him, the way seemed long. But the sky was bright, and he somehow felt he was headed in the right direction" (*Stuart Little* 131).

Some controversy arose after the publication of *Stuart Little*. Anne Carroll Moore, a retired librarian from the New York Public Library, sent White a letter in which she adamantly recommended that the book not be reprinted again. She called the idea that a human woman could give birth to a mouse monstrous and grotesque. She was not the only one who protested. White became upset, since he hadn't meant to imply as much. In fact, in the book, he introduces Stuart as "the baby looked very much like a mouse" (*Stuart Little* 1). Truthfully, though, several incidents in the book do refer to Stuart as a mouse. However, in a letter to his editor, Ursula Nordstrom (who hired Garth Williams to illustrate both *Stuart Little* and later *Charlotte's Web*), White explains, "Nowhere in the book (I think

I am right about this) is Stuart described as a mouse. He is a small guy who *looks* very much like a mouse, but he obviously is not a mouse. He is a second son." After some apparent investigation, he adds, "I am wrong. Stuart *is* called a mouse on Page 36—I just found it. He should not have been."[23] The public protest continued, and in subsequent editions of the book, White changed the word "born" in the opening sentence to "arrived."

Another criticism of the book came from the fact that the story has an open ending. With Stuart disappearing down the road, still away from his family and still searching for his lovely bird, Margalo, the reader can't be sure what ultimately happens. Throughout the years, White defended this ambiguity, stating that "Stuart's journey symbolizes the continuing journey that everybody takes, in search of what is perfect and unattainable." White never changed the ending, instead remaining true to giving his readers what he whole-heartedly believed, that life is a continual voyage. Many years after it first appeared in print, White responded to a fan who had asked about the ending of the book:

> Stuart Little is the story of a quest, or search. Much of life is questing and searching, and I was writing about that. If the book ends while the search is still going on, that's because I wanted it that way. As you grow older you will realize that many of us in this world go through life looking for something that seems beautiful and good—often something we can't quite name. In Stuart's case, he was searching for the bird Margalo, who was his ideal of beauty and goodness. Whether he ever found her or not, or whether he ever got home or not, is less important than the adventure itself. If the book made you cry, that's because you are aware of the sadness and richness of life's involvements and of the quest for beauty.[24]

The book itself doesn't unfold in the traditional fashion, but is rather told in short scenes of Stuart's adventures—from getting caught in the lampshade to being carried off on top of a garbage heap to the East River. White wanted the book to offer children the chance to pick it up and dive in at any time, regardless of what chapter they choose to open. Thus, the book contains fifteen short sketches that could feasibly be read in any order and still come across as individual, self-contained stories.

Aside from these slight criticisms, *Stuart Little* received mostly positive reviews and was hailed as a book enjoyable for both children and adults because of its humor and the absence of the sentimentality often found in books written for a young audience. It is ironic to note that *Stuart Little* is considered one of White's funniest works, though he wrote it during a time when he struggled with depression brought on by fears about his health, the health of Katharine, the threat of nuclear war after World War II, and the general anxiety that would plague him for the remainder of his life.

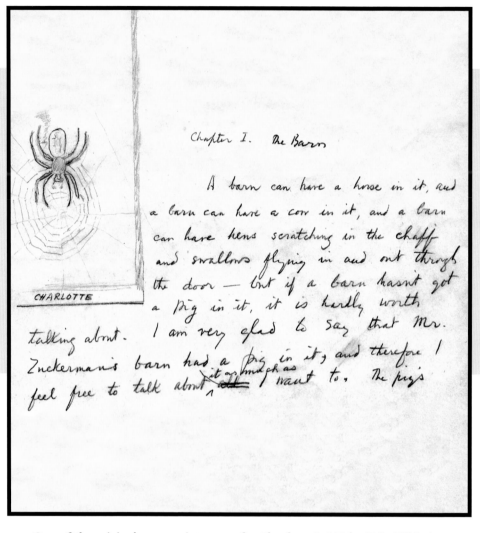

Chapter I. The Barn

A barn can have a horse in it, and a barn can have a cow in it, and a barn can have hens scratching in the chaff and swallows flying in and out through the door — but if a barn hasn't got a pig in it, it is hardly worth talking about. I am very glad to say that Mr. Zuckerman's barn had a pig in it, and therefore I feel free to talk about it as much as I want to. The pig's

CHARLOTTE

One of the original manuscript pages for Charlotte's Web, *E.B. White's most popular book and one of the most beloved books of all time. Most of the novel was written from April to October 1950 in a sparsely furnished boathouse that was the exact size as Thoreau's cabin at Walden Pond!* Charlotte's Web *was the number-one book in the "Teacher's Top 100 Books," as compiled by the National Education Association in 1999.*

6

A Very Good Friend Indeed

FOR THE NEXT several years, White and Katharine remained in New York, living in Manhattan in an apartment at 229 East Forty-eighth Street. White continued to fight his lingering depression, though he had bouts of happiness on the occasional visits the family made to Maine. He managed to produce work for *The New Yorker*, though his columns appeared less and less frequently. He just didn't have the energy or inspiration to write as he used to. In 1948, White received honorary degrees from the University of Maine, Yale University, and Dartmouth College for his contributions to the literary world. As the year unfolded, he slowly regained some of his zest for writing, producing three of his best essays, "The Second Tree from the Corner," "Death of a Pig," and "Here is New York."

The essay "Death of a Pig" sprung from a real-life event that would eventually inspire White to compose his second children's book. In the autobiographical piece, White recounts his struggle to rescue a sick pig, staying up several nights to take care of it. Unfortunately, his efforts failed and the pig died despite the round-the-clock care White gave him. But from this episode sprang something positive, the idea for another children's book. White had been contemplating the idea of composing another one for a few years and even had some pages stashed in a drawer somewhere. In January 1951, he wrote his editor to see if she would be interested in reading it.

In a letter to a fan, Mrs. Kaston, White later explained the impetus for *Charlotte's Web*:

> The idea of the writing in *Charlotte's Web* came to me one day when I was on my way down through the orchard carrying a pail of slops to my pig. I had made up my mind to write a children's book about animals, and I needed a way to save a pig's life, and I had been watching a large spider in the backhouse, and what with one thing and another, the idea came to me.[25]

Not much is known about the actual writing process of the book that became *Charlotte's Web*. The first drafts, written on notebook paper in pencil, appeared hastily scribbled and much edited along the way. The bulk of the novel seems to be written in the months spanning April to October 1950. White spent his time during those days in a sparsely furnished boathouse in Maine, equipped simply with a typewriter, clean paper, chair, bench, wastebasket, and stove. The boathouse was near the sea and was the exact same size as the cabin belonging to Thoreau at Walden Pond—ten by fifteen feet.

White created the character of the spider Charlotte to embody the true attributes of these arachnids, which do trap, kill, and eat their prey. At the same time, he made her a sympathetic character. In the book, Charlotte explains her nature in a way that makes it clear that she is just behaving the way she was made:

> I am not entirely happy about my diet of flies and bugs, but it's the way I'm made. A spider has to pick up a living some-how or other, and I happen to be a trapper. I just naturally build a web and trap flies and other insects. My mother was a trapper before me. Her mother was a trapper before her. All our family have been trappers. Way back for thousands and thousands of years we spiders have been laying for flies and bugs. (*Charlotte's Web* 39)

In writing *Charlotte's Web*, White paid close attention to the anatomical and scientific truthfulness of the spider's body and life. At first, White named the spider of his story Charlotte Epeira, giving her the Latin name for Grey Cross spider. Just to be sure he had the right species, White climbed up a ladder to the corner of his barn where his real spider companion had spun her web. He discovered that she was in fact a different species. White quickly renamed her character, altering it to the more scientifically accurate "Charlotte A. Cavatica."

The story-telling approach in *Charlotte's Web* differs from the whimsical nature of *Stuart Little*. Aside from the fact that the central characters are animals and insects who converse and interact with one another, the story remains close to the details of farm life. At the heart of the story is the ever-present danger faced by members of the barnyard; mainly, the looming threat of imminent slaughter for cows, chickens, and, in this particular story, pigs. That is the specter that awaits Wilbur, the ever-fatter, somewhat melancholy pig who Charlotte strives to save. White tried hard to combine the realistic aspects with the fantastical. He wanted very much to remain true to the natural behavior of the animals and to the situation on the farm, in particular the age-old conflict between humans and animals.

> A farm is a peculiar problem for a man who likes animals, because the fate of most livestock is that they are murdered by their benefactors. The creatures may live serenely but they end violently, and the odor of doom hangs about them always. . . . I do not like to betray a person or a creature, and I tend to agree with Mr. E.M. Forster that in these times the duty of a man, above all else, is to be reliable. It used to be clear to me, slopping a pig, that as far as the pig was concerned I could not be counted on, and this, as I say, troubled me. Anyway, the theme of *Charlotte's Web* is that a pig shall be saved, and I have an idea that somewhere deep inside me there was a wish to that effect.[26]

In the initial draft, White started the story with a description of Wilbur, a newborn runt pig who arrives at the Arable family's farm, and his pig pen. As he worked on the book, White realized that he'd have to introduce the human protagonists earlier in the story. He wanted readers to meet the central human, Fern Arable, who first rescues Wilbur from the deadly slice of a blade. His first opening turned into Chapter 3 in the book, and White began the book

Wilbur, Geoffrey, and Templeton gather to admire the magical weaving of Charlotte in a scene from the 1973 animated film of Charlotte's Web. *A small inset shows the book cover for* Charlotte's Web, *designed by Garth Williams.*

instead with a beginning he hoped would capture and hold the reader's interest: "'Where's Papa going with that axe?' said Fern to her mother as they were setting the table for breakfast" (*Charlotte's Web* 1).

Throughout the book, White relied on his own memory and experiences on the farm, harkening back to his life as a child. His descriptions of farm life in the novel ring true and vivid, and mirror White's love for that world:

> The barn was pleasantly warm in winter when the animals spent most of their time indoors, and it was pleasantly cool in summer when the big doors stood wide open to the breeze. The barn had stalls on the main floor for the work horses, tie-ups on the main floor for the cows, a sheepfold down below for the sheep, a pigpen down below for Wilbur, and it was full of all sorts of things that you find in barns: ladders, grindstones, pitch forks, monkey wrenches, scythes, lawn mowers, snow shovels, ax handles, milk pails, water buckets, empty grain sacks, and rusty rat traps. It was the kind of barn that swallows like to build their nests in. It was the kind of barn that children like to play in. (*Charlotte's Web* 13–14)

In the novel, as soon as the soft-hearted eight-year-old Fern learns that her father intends to kill Wilbur because he is the runt, she races out to the barn, begging him to let her take care of the littlest pig in the litter. Seeing Fern's great despair, her father finally agrees, and she spends the next five weeks bottle-feeding the steadily growing Wilbur until he is too round and fat to hold in her arms or to fit in the wood house outside under an apple tree. Fern's family finally convinces her it is in Wilbur's best interest that he be sold to Uncle Zuckerman, who lives on a nearby farm, where the pig can roam freely in his own wooden pen.

Even though Fern visits Wilbur every day after school, he finds himself lonely in the barn with only the cranky rat Templeton and the nearby (and slightly irritating) lambs and geese for company. He spends his days feeling sorry for himself, wallowing in the mud, and chowing down on a steady and fattening diet of "skim milk, provender, leftover sandwich from Lurvy's lunchbox, prune skins, a morsel of this, a bit of that, fried potatoes, marmalade drippings, a little more of this, a little more of that, a piece of baked apple, a scrap of upside-down cake" (*Charlotte's Web* 26). Then one night after Wilbur has nearly given up on finding some comfort and a friend to play with, "out of the darkness, came a small voice he had never heard before. It sounded rather thin, but pleasant. 'Do you want a friend, Wilbur?' it said. 'I'll be a friend to you. . . . I've watched you all day and I like you'" (*Charlotte's Web* 31). The voice belongs to Charlotte and from the beginning their relationship serves as an education and ultimately a life-saver for Wilbur. When Wilbur receives the devastating news that he will be put to death in the spring, Charlotte comes up with the idea to spin the words "Some Pig" in her web. As soon as Mr. Zuckerman caught sight of those words sparkling in the web above Wilbur's head,

Did you know...

Charlotte's Web was inspired by E.B. White's love of a rural life. He had observed spiders up close and was drawn to their intricate webs. White tried several approaches to *Charlotte's Web* before he felt that he had gotten the atmosphere of life on the farm just right. Inklings of the foundation for the story can be found in his essay "Death of a Pig," which was published first in the *Atlantic Monthly* in January 1948 and was later part of a larger collection, *The Second Tree From the Corner*.

he viewed it as a miracle and evidence that Wilbur truly is a strange and wondrous creature. The news spreads, and soon the farmyard fills with people from all over the country who have come to witness this fabulous pig. Next, Charlotte spins "Terrific!" and later "Radiant!" Charlotte's trick buys Wilbur time, but Charlotte must again work her magic when Mr. Zuckerman hauls Wilbur to the county fair to be bought and killed. Charlotte hides in Wilbur's carrying box, and before dawn, she has exhausted herself spinning another message: "Humble." Her plan works; the Zuckermans are finally convinced that Wilbur is a pig worth keeping.

In Charlotte, White builds a character who may be a carnivore, but who also embodies intelligence, empathy, and creativity. She not only saves Wilbur, but she helps him to grow up and even teaches him how to face the hardest and most inevitable part of the life cycle: death. Near the end of the book, when she realizes that she will die after laying her eggs, Charlotte says to Wilbur, "After all, what's a life anyway? We're born, we live a little, we die. A spider's life can't help being something of a mess, with all this trapping and eating flies. By helping you, perhaps I was trying to lift up my life a trifle. Heaven knows anyone's life can stand a little of that" (*Charlotte's Web* 164). Though the news of her death crushes Wilbur, he manages to stow her egg sack in his pen, return to the barn, and, in the springtime, he watches as hundreds of her children hatch and make their way into the world.

As in *Stuart Little*, White refused to condescend to children by writing a sweet little fairy tale where the story ends with a concrete "happily-ever-after." At the same time, the ending of *Charlotte's Web* shows White's enduring faith in the importance of memory and the lasting nature of love.

"Wilbur never forgot Charlotte. Although he loved her children and grandchildren dearly, none of the new spiders ever quite took her place in his heart. She was in a class by herself. It is not often that someone comes along who is a true friend and a good writer. Charlotte was both" (*Charlotte's Web* 184).

Published on October 15, 1952, to excellent reviews, the book became an instant classic. The well-known Southern writer Eudora Welty, reviewing *Charlotte's Web* in the *Sunday New York Times Book Review*, wrote that "the book has grace and humor and praise of life and the good backbone of succinctness that only the most highly imaginative stories grow. . . . It is about life and death, trust and treachery, pleasure and pain, and the passing of time. . . . As a piece of work it is just about perfect."[27]

As of 1995, the book had sold more than six million copies. Even today, it continues to be included on the list of ten best books for children, along with such other well-loved and popular books as *Tom Sawyer, Little Women, The Little House on the Prairie, The Wizard of Oz*, and *The Island of the Blue Dolphins*.

Despite his worldly successes, including being awarded the Presidential Medal of Freedom and honorary degrees from seven universities, E.B. White appeared to like life on his farm the best. White is shown here playing baseball with his granddaughter Martha in 1960.

7

Living in Style

IN 1951, HAROLD Ross, the long-time editor and close friend of the Whites, died. Both Katharine and White were devastated by the news. They continued to work for *The New Yorker*, Katharine as the editor of the Fiction Department and White as a contributing writer, but their experience at the magazine was never the same after Ross's death. The financial success of *Charlotte's Web*, however, allowed White to concentrate more thoroughly on a collection of his essays, called *The Second Tree from the Corner*. In the foreword of the book, he describes it as "a book of revelations:

essays, poems, stories, opinions, reports, drawn from the past, the present, the future, the city" (*Second Tree from the Corner* xi). The book appeared in print on January 1954 and again the writing met with praise from the critics.

White lived in Maine from April to October 1954. The year was a productive one for his writing, both the weekly contributions to "Notes and Comments" for *The New Yorker* and other essays. At times, his focus in "Notes and Comments" illustrated a somber tone unlike the humorous bent of his children's books and the various satirical pieces he'd written over the years. He used the column to offer his perspective on issues such as war, the United Nations, the pollution of the atmosphere from testing atomic weapons, and McCarthyism. When he had a strong opinion, he was not afraid to put it into words, even if that meant criticizing the policies of men like Senator Joseph McCarthy and his investigation of so-called Communist spies in the State Department.

The year 1954 brought White several more honors, such as honorary degrees from Harvard University and Colby College. He was also delighted to be asked by *Yale Review* to compose an essay in honor of the 100th anniversary of the publication of Thoreau's *Walden*, perhaps the one book White cherished most and whose philosophy he closely attempted to follow. White described his experience writing the essay to his friend Daise Terry, "Have just written a piece for the *Yale Review* on the subject of *Walden* and am having nightmares from the fear that I have plagiarized myself. At my age, Miss T., a writer repeats like an onion."[28]

White was fifty-five and Katharine sixty-two when they decided to finally make the trip to England that they had promised each other years before. The trip turned out to be more difficult than they anticipated, in part because of White's fears of driving on the left side of the road and by what the Whites perceived as the haughty nature of people at the Connaught Hotel in London, where they were staying. White also felt concern over a possible worker's strike by the stewards on the ocean liner they were to take home. Though they had planned to meet their son Joel, his wife Allene, and their three children in Germany where Joel was stationed, the Whites agreed they didn't feel they could remain overseas. White writes of the experience to a friend as being "a mild and uncomfortable excursion into ineptitude, during which I felt at all times unsuitably dressed and unable to speak properly."[29] Three weeks into what was initially meant to be a longer journey, Katharine and White once again (and gratefully) set foot in New York City.

As the year progressed, Katharine became less interested in working at *The New Yorker* without Ross at her side. White stopped writing his "Notes and Comments" pieces in the fall of 1955, concentrating instead on several loosely connected essays that eventually were published as *The Points of My Compass*. Physically, White had never felt worse. He suffered from stomach trouble so severe that he had an x-ray and tests done in January 1956 to determine the problem. The doctor diagnosed the condition as "pylorus," which basically meant that the stomach muscle closed off when White was in distress.

Good news came in the form of the return of Joel, Allene, and their children back to the United States. They moved near the White's farm in Maine, which allowed White and Katharine the opportunity to visit them from the city with greater frequency.

Finally, in May 1957, Katharine relinquished her job as fiction editor at *The New Yorker*. Between October and November, the Whites moved their belongings from their winter place in Turtle Bay Gardens, New York, where they had periodically stayed for fifteen years, to their farm on Allen Cove. White felt as though he had finally come home to stay.

White wasted no time in restocking the barnyard. He bought two Hereford heifers, sheep, chickens, geese, and steers. He could now rise with the sun and begin his daily chores of feeding, gardening, and making repairs or building projects around the farm without shouldering the weight of regular writing deadlines from *The New Yorker* that he'd had for thirty years. He owned a new boat called *Fern* and could sail aboard its twenty-foot deck whenever he had a free moment. Now he could write whenever he had the urge and on whatever subject he pleased. His writing moments were spent away from the clamor of the house in the secluded boathouse, where he could listen to the sounds of the animals in the forest and the faint, rhythmic sound of the waves from the pond hitting the shore.

In the meantime, an old friend at Cornell sent him a copy of their former instructor's textbook for English 8, the rules that their professor William Strunk, Jr., had impressed on them in English class in 1918. Happy to be reminded of the text, White wrote an essay called "Will Strunk" for *The New Yorker*, extolling the virtues of his former teacher's sound advice on writing and style. Jack Case, an editor at Macmillan Publishing Company, read the essay and subsequently asked White to use it for an introduction to the book, *The Elements of Style*, which Macmillan wanted to publish. White agreed under the stipulation that he could revise the initial essay. The editor reassured him that a revision would be acceptable and also asked him to take a look at the text of Strunk's book. At first, White thought revising the ideas of his old professor would prove easy. He soon found that some of Strunk's ideas weren't supported by enough clear examples and that others were murky. He remained committed, though, to keeping the heart of Strunk's advice and design.

> My single purpose is to be faithful to Strunk as of 1958, reliable, holding the line and maybe even selling some copies to English Departments that collect oddities and curios. To me no cause is lost, no level the right level, no smooth ride as valuable as a rough ride, no *like* interchangeable with *as*, and no ball game anything but chaotic if it lacks a mound, a box, bases, and foul lines. That's what Strunk was about, that's what I am about, and that (I hope) is what the book is about. Any attempt to tamper with this prickly design will get nobody nowhere fast.[30]

Though he was ill at the time, White finished revising his introductory essay and the text a day before his Thanksgiving

Did you know...

In his own writing, E.B. White tried very hard to adhere to rule number thirteen of Strunk and White's *The Elements of Style*: "Omit needless words." In both his children's books and his essays, White often revised again and again, ruthlessly cutting out words that made the writing less concise. In an interview, White explained that "The main thing I try to do is write as clearly as I can."

deadline in November 1958. His essay illustrated the components of style that he recommended; it was clear, concise, conversational and humorous in tone, and practical. The book became the Book-of-the-Month pick for May 1959 and has remained a best-seller for years. Today, many high school and university teachers use Strunk and White's *The Elements of Style* as a primary text to teach clear and concise writing.

Life in Maine continued fairly happily for the Whites. Though Katharine reduced her long-distance editing tasks to one-third, she remained busy with keeping up with White's and her heavy correspondence load. White frequently received letters from school children, asking about Stuart, Charlotte, or Wilbur, and he and Katharine were committed to responding to their readers, even when more letter writing than essay writing got done. To a batch of letters from Mrs. Bard's fifth graders who were worried that White had retired from writing children's books, White offered a reassuring reply, "I don't know where you got the idea I was retiring. I don't intend ever to do that. But if I don't stop answering letters I'll never get another book written."[31] One boy from Newton High School even asked White's advice on a report the student was writing on White. White responded to the boy's questions about style in typical tongue-in-cheek manner:

> I am a confused writer at 25 West 43 Street, and one of the reasons for my confusion is that students want me to explain myself. I can't explain myself. Everything about me is mysterious to me and I do not make any very strong effort to solve the puzzle. If you are engaged in writing a theme about my works, I think your best bet is to read them and say what you think about them.

The question of "style" is a vexing one, always. No sensible writer sets out deliberately to develop a style, but all writers do have distinguishing qualities, and they become very evident when you read the words. Take Hemingway and Willa Cather —two well-known American novelists. The first is extremely self-conscious and puts himself into every sentence and every situation; the seconds is largely self-effacing and loses herself completely in the lives of her characters.[32]

One thing was sure, White loved their white clapboard house and everything associated with it. He loved the surrounding land, the cows in the pasture, the bleating of the sheep mixed with the honking of geese, and the easy trip from the house to the boat dock. During the summer months and on weekends, he and Katharine spent much of their time with Nancy and Roger, Katharine's two children from her first marriage, and Joel, his wife Allene, and their three young children. In an essay for *The New Yorker*, he wrote of those days with fondness:

> I have only three grandchildren, and one of them can't walk in the woods, because he was only born on June 24th last and hasn't managed to get onto his feet yet. But he has been making some good tries, and when he does walk, the woods are what he will head for if he is anything like his brother Steven and his sister Martha, and, of course, me. . . . We walk in them at every opportunity, stumble along happily, tripping over windfalls, sniffing valerian, and annoying the jay. We note where the deer has lain under the wild apple, and we watch the red squirrel shucking spruce buds.[33]

In fact, White wrote occasionally for *The New Yorker*, and his pieces, as they had during World War II and McCarthyism, continued to contain political elements. One of his primary causes between 1959 and 1960 concerned environmental pollution. As always, White wrote not only to entertain, but also to instruct and, most importantly, to make people aware of what was occurring in the world around them.

In his personal life, White had more concrete concerns: his health and that of Katharine's. Both the Whites struggled with illness over the years, but Katharine, seven years older than White, was diagnosed in 1957 as having a blockage in her right carotid artery. She needed immediate surgery at Strong Memorial Hospital in Rochester, New York. From the surgery up until she died in 1977, Katharine would fight bouts of illness that often left her bedridden, out of breath, and in pain. The same year of Katharine's surgery, James Thurber, White's long-time friend and fellow *New Yorker* collaborator, passed away from a brain tumor. White helped to put together Thurber's eulogy, calling Thurber "both a practitioner of humor and a defender of it. . . . Once, I remember, he heard someone say that humor is a shield, and it made him mad. He wasn't going to have anyone beatings his sword into a shield. . . . During his happiest years, Thurber did not write the way a surgeon operates, he wrote the way a child skips rope, the way a mouse waltzes."[34]

Seeing his wife age and struggle, feeling the distant ache of arthritis in his bones, and losing his lifelong friends caused White great anxiety and depression. Despite this, he published *The Points of My Compass*, a collection of his essays from *The New Yorker* in the fall of 1962, just in time for Katharine's birthday. However, other than this collection, White found himself unable to write. Katharine had retired from her editorial duties at *The New Yorker* in January 1961 after thirty-five years of service, so they no longer had her income from those assignments. Fearing that Katharine's declining health would require the additional expense of nurses, caretakers, and hospital visits, White began to worry about their finances. Financial anxiety haunted him even when he received nationwide recognition of his talent and fame, as he did in 1963, when White was given a Presidential Medal of Freedom from President John F. Kennedy. On good days, White wrote for pleasure. On bad days, he wrote out of fear.

A close-up of the head of a Canadian trumpeter swan, the beautiful animal E.B. White built his novel The Trumpet of the Swan *around. Published in 1970, the novel became a best-seller for White. In 1971, he received the National Medal for Literature for his contribution to American literary life.*

8

Without a Voice

LOUIS IS A Canadian trumpeter swan with a disability. Unlike his peers, he is physically unable to make the "ko-hoh" sound to speak to them or to make the mating call. Because of this problem, Louis feels that he will never be able to capture the attention of Serena, the female swan with whom he has fallen in love. Luckily, Louis meets Sam Beaver, an eleven-year-old boy who becomes his friend, even taking him to school where Louis, sitting among the children, learns to read and write on a black slate so he can communicate with humans. Not knowing what else to do to help his son, Louis's father breaks a window of a music store and steals a trumpet, which Louis learns to play and to use as a way to speak the language of the swans. However, Louis wants to pay back the music store for the broken window and the trumpet, and so he (like Stuart Little) sets out on a journey. He entertains boat passengers in Boston and plays in night-clubs in Philadelphia, steadily making back the money by playing the trumpet. One night, Serena appears at the pond in the zoo where Louis is staying. She falls in love with him and the two fly back to Montana together.

White started *The Trumpet of the Swan* in 1968, though, as with *Stuart Little*, he had previously jotted down notes about the story. Part of why he wrote the book was in response to Katharine's poor health and his own haunting fear of dying soon.

White had never actually seen a real trumpeter swan, but he felt compelled to write the book. For one thing, the trumpeter swan was on the endangered species list. For another, White, almost seventy years old, wanted to write a book that would reflect the days of his youth. In addition, White wrote to a friend that the book was inspired for other (more practical) reasons. "I'm glad you liked my kooky swan story. . . . I'll tackle anything in a pinch, and I began to feel the pinch more than a year ago when I looked around and discovered that my house was full of day nurses and night nurses at $28 per day. Or night. It runs into money fast."[35]

He knew the Philadelphia Zoo kept such birds on Bird Lake, and so White wrote his old travelling friend, Howard Cushman, to ask for his assistance on his newest project.

> How would you like to do some sleuthing for an aging fiction writer? It would take you, on these golden October days,

season of mists and mellow fruitiness, to the Zoological Gardens, there to scan birds and maybe even grill a curator. One of my fictional characters has had the rotten nerve to take me to Philly, and I am severely handicapped, having only been to your quaint burg twice in my life—once in 1920 or 1921 to squire Alice Burchfield to a Penn game, and once in the Fifties to watch the Giants.[36]

He requested that Cush send him photographs and asked him a series of questions about the birds. How many baby swans had hatched that year? Do the swans spend all their time in the water? How are the birds held captive? Being a life-long animal lover, White already knew some things about swans, which he skillfully weaved into the story. Readers learn that it takes the mother swan thirty-five days to hatch her eggs, that a male swan is called a "cob," that babies are "cygnets," and that the female swan is known as a "pen." At times, his information was very specific:

> A little swan enclosed in an egg has a hard time getting out. It never would get out if Nature had not provided it with two important things: a powerful neck-muscle and a small dagger-tooth on the tip of its bill. This tooth is sharp and the baby swan uses it to pick a hole in the tough shell of the egg. Once the hole is made, the rest is easy. The cygnet can breathe now; it just keeps wiggling until it wiggles free. (*The Trumpet of the Swan* 30)

And though he hadn't ever even seen a trumpeter swan in real life, he did remember seeing swans in the wilderness. The scenes at Camp Kookooskoos were written with Camp Otter in mind, a place in Ontario where White was a summer counselor in 1920 and 1921.

For White, the book was a love story between Louis and Serena, but also an adventure tale about two boys growing up and on the brink of independence. It is also a story about the relationship between Louis and his father, who wants what is best for his son but is not sure how to help him.

Like his other two previous children's books, there are many similarities between the characters in *The Trumpet of the Swan* and White himself. First of all, White understood Louis's difficulties in communicating, because he knew intimately the feeling of being unable to speak. As a boy, he hated speaking in front of his classmates and as an adult he often refused to appear in public, even to accept awards or honorary degrees from universities. Also, White remembered his stumbling inability to talk to girls in the same way that Louis the swan has trouble

Did you know...

Five years before White published *The Trumpet of the Swan*, he sent a letter to his friend Howard Cushman dated July 21, 1965. His words hint that his interest in trumpeter swans had been piqued long before he sat down to write the manuscript. He wrote: "If I get to Philly in the near future it will be because I am irresistibly drawn to your Zoo's bird park, where, as you probably don't know, a pair of trumpeter swans (with an assist from a second female) recently hatched five cygnets. I have never seen a trumpeter swan, and this would be my chance. *The N.Y. Times* had a lovely pix of them."

speaking to his love, Serena. And lastly, the central idea of music as a way to communicate echoes White's memories of his father, a piano repairman, musician, and president of the Walters Piano Company, who made sure their home was filled with music.

The human boy, Sam Beaver, also shares characteristics of the writer, particularly the serenity of being in the wilderness. "Sam always felt happy when he was in a place among wild creatures. Sitting on his log, watching the swans, he had the same good feeling some people get when they're sitting in church" (*The Trumpet of the Swan* 22). Sam, like White, keeps a notebook where he records many things: the events of the day, his thoughts, and questions about why things happen the way that they do. And through Sam, White is able to share the joy he remembered from the trips his family used to take every summer to the Belgrade Lakes in Maine as well as the fears he had at that age:

> But the thing he enjoyed most in life was these camping trips in Canada with his father. They would motor to the border and cross into Canada. There Mr. Beaver would hire a bush pilot to fly them to the lake where his camp was, for a few days of fishing and loafing and exploring. . . . These were the pleasantest days of Sam's life, these days in the woods, far, far from everywhere—no automobiles, no roads, no people, no noise, no school, no homework, no problems, except the problem of getting lost. And, of course, the problem of what to be when he grew up. Every boy has *that* problem. (*The Trumpet of the Swan* 5)

White rushed the manuscript of *The Trumpet of the Swan* to his publishers in November 1969, certain that he would die before he saw it in print. Because he was in such a hurry to send it to the publishers, he didn't have time to ask Garth Williams to illustrate the book, as he had for *Stuart Little* and *Charlotte's Web*. He wrote of his regrets to Williams in 1969, stating that he had "always hoped that Williams and White would be as indestructible as ham and eggs, Scotch and soda, Gilbert and Sullivan."[37] Instead, Fred Marcellino was commissioned to draw the pictures for the book.

Critics reacted less favorably to White's third children's book, saying that it was not equal to the work of an established writer of White's stature. White, too, found fault with the book, feeling that it was too long and too hastily written. However, critics also noted its wit and humor. John Updike's review in the June 1970 issue of *The New York Times Book Review* called it a book in which "the simplicity never condescends, the straight and earnest telling that happens upon, rather than veers into comedy . . . [the book is] an accumulation of preposterous particulars" that "engenders textures of small surprise and delightful rightness."[38]

White needn't have worried about the commercial success of the novel; the book, like its predecessors, became an enduring best-seller. In 1971, it went to the number one slot on *The New York Times* bestseller list for children, with *Charlotte's Web* hanging strong at number two on the list. The Philadelphia Orchestra asked permission to perform the story in music to raise money for the Philadelphia Zoo. White was amazed by this honor, writing to a friend about how strange it was to think of his book turned into a musical. "Imagine me, sitting down there in my boathouse a year and a half ago, composing the lines of Sam Beaver's poem and not having the slightest inkling that the Philadelphia Orchestra was tuning up onstage. What a life I lead! How Merry! How innocent! How nutty!"[39] In addition, a placard was placed in front of a trumpeter swan display at the Philadelphia Zoo that named it the place Louis and Serena had fallen in love.

The following years brought White several great honors. In 1970, White was recognized for his achievements in children's literature by receiving an award from the Laura Ingalls Wilder Foundation. In 1971, he received the National Medal for Literature. And in 1978, the advisory board for the Pulitzer Prize gave White a special citation. Because of his shyness, White didn't attend any of the ceremonies. Instead, he sent gracious notes of gratitude in his place.

Though White didn't write as much as he used to, he did continue to work on several different projects. He started on a revision of Strunk and White's *The Elements of Style*, though he often suffered from spells of dizziness that made him have to put aside the project every once in awhile. He also assisted on the screenplay to the movie of *Charlotte's Web* that was in production. He wrote many letters to those involved in the project offering suggestions. His main concern was that the animals in the film should act like animals, not people. He wanted to be sure that the tale remained true to what he had in mind, a portrayal of life on the farm as realistic and respectful as possible. When the movie was released, White was extremely displeased with it. He didn't like that they added music and that they made the portion of Fern's crush on Henry such a large part of the story. He also objected to the fact that the movie made the book into a moral tale. He clearly stated his position in a letter to J.G. Gude: "As I look back on the screenplay, it strikes me that not enough is placed in the barn and the animals and the web, and this results in quite a buildup of Henry Fussy and boy-meets-girl. *Charlotte's Web* is not a boy-girl story, it is a study of miracles, tinged with the faint but pervasive odor of the barn. It will stand or fall on the barn." [40]

In the meantime, White's goddaughter, Dorothy Lobrano Guth, suggested that White publish a collection of his letters. Being a fairly private person, White was at first unsure about letting the world so intimately into his personal life. However, he finally agreed to the undertaking. White, who could never seem to throw anything away, had saved up many of his rough drafts of the hundreds of letters he'd sent over the decades, along with letters he had gotten from family, friends, and fans. For four years, he, Katharine, and Dorothy sifted through the boxes and boxes of correspondence he had saved, and in November 1976, *Letters of E.B. White* was published. Both he and Katharine had been very responsible in answering as many fan letters as possible. Often, readers wrote White asking for writing advice, and he always tried to give them something useful. To one writer, he responded by illuminating his own writing process:

> I've yet to see the book that was effortless to write. They all take it out of you, one way or another. . . . If you are at the moment struggling with a book, what you should ask yourself is, 'Do I really care about this particular set of characters, this thing I am doing?' If you do, then nothing should deter you. If you are doubtful about it, then I'd turn to something else. I knew in the case of Charlotte, that I cared deeply about the whole bunch of them. So I went ahead. . . . May good luck go with you. [41]

White, even after having published seventeen books, felt a lot like his swan, Louis. Self-expression was difficult, and it was often only through the art of writing that he was able to feel that he truly could find his voice. He had spent most of his lifetime searching for the right words to say what he really meant.

As someone who wrote for one of the most sophisticated and cosmopolitan magazines and yet kept a childlike wonderment and curiosity about the natural world, E.B. White's life presents a fascinating contrast.

9

A Man Who Loved the World

ON THE MORNING of July 20, 1977, Katharine was rushed to the hospital. It was not the first time she had been taken in; she had suffered from congestive heart failure on their forty-sixth anniversary in 1975. Over the last few years, her eyes had begun to fail and she needed a walker to move around the house. One of her greatest pleasures, diving into a book, became impossible because of her loss of sight. She could no longer do the editing she loved or help to answer the many fan letters that arrived daily. Even her voice began to wane and she often became cranky or impatient because of the constant pain she experienced. The night of July 20, White stayed by her side, holding her hand until her heart slowed and finally stopped. In a letter to a friend, he writes of the experience, saying that he "sat on a small stool just inside the door of the Intensive Care Unit and watched the heart monitor send its tiny, bright signals of doom."[42]

Before her death, Katharine had been very specific about what she wanted. Neither she nor White were very religious, and so she requested there be no church funeral. Instead, she wanted a small graveside ceremony with only her family in attendance. Though all of her children and grandchildren came to the service, White was so grief stricken at her death that he couldn't bring himself to go and say good-bye to her that way. White tried to put into words the loss that he felt at the house empty of her buoyant presence. "I have lost the one thing that seemed to make any sense in my life, and I feel like a child lost at Coney Island."[43] Though he knew she was gone, a part of him always entered their farmhouse half-expecting to find her there. "When I'm upstairs, it's easy to believe K.'s somewhere down there. When I'm downstairs I'll lulled into thinking she is up in the bedroom."[44]

White knew of Katharine's love of the garden. At one point, he bought her a greenhouse so that she could care for the flowers and small shrubs as much as she liked. After her death, he visited her grave every day; taking her flowers and planting an oak tree nearby the gravestone to give it shade. Two years later, he even published a book of her garden articles that had appeared in *The New Yorker*. He titled the book *Onward and Upward in the Garden*. In the introduction of the book, White wrote a sketch of his wife that illustrated her love of the outdoors and caring for the flowers there:

> Armed with a diagram and a clipboard, Katharine would get
> into a shabby old Brooks raincoat much too long for her . . .

and proceed to the director's chair. . . . There she would sit, hour after hour, in the wind and the weather, while Henry Allen produced dozens of brown paper packages of new bulbs and a basketful of old ones, ready for the intricate interment. As the years went by and age overtook her, there was something comical yet touching in her bedraggled appearance on this awesome occasion—the small, hunched-over figure, her studied absorption in the implausible notion that there would be yet another spring, oblivious to the ending of her own days, which she knew perfectly well was near at hand, sitting there with her detailed chart under those dark skies in the dying October, calmly plotting the resurrection.[45]

Onward and Upward in the Garden received critical praise and was read not just by gardeners, but by general readers as well.

White continually struggled with his declining health. He still suffered from the hay fever he'd had since he was a child and his joints were creaky with arthritis. More than anything, he felt lonely without Katharine. He had never

Did you know...

Throughout his lifetime, E.B. White maintained a clear sense of political integrity. Many of his essays dealt with important issues of the day in a clear, matter-of-fact way. White openly discussed many controversial topics including the effectiveness of democracy, censorship, pollution, the right to privacy, and the tax system of the Internal Revenue Service (IRS). His humorous, tongue-in-cheek writing allowed him to be critical and polite at the same time.

been a very social person, and she was the one who brought people and a sense of liveliness to the house. Now that she was gone, White, whose friendships were few by then, since many of his friends were dead or dying, very seldom invited people over.

One friend who was still alive and who now spent time with White arranging his literary life was Corona Macheme, an editor at Harper and Row who had helped him in the putting together of *Letters*. She started to help him sort out, from the hundreds of odds and ends, pieces that he had collected over the years, poems and small pieces to be published in a compilation. Together, they went through piece after piece, sorting them into boxes marked Yes, No, and Maybe. White kept throwing things in the No box, and Corona kept taking them out. Finally, they had pieced together enough stories and poems to publish a book called *Poems and Sketches of E.B. White*. The two became closer, vacationing together in Sarasota, Florida, in the spring of 1980 and taking a camping trip on White's eighty-first birthday. To celebrate, they went to Great Pond in Maine, where White had received a green canoe from his dad on his eleventh birthday. Though Corona was a friend and not a replacement for Katharine in White's heart, her company did help to brighten his days. He wrote to a friend in 1982 that "the pleasure of Corona's company in these last difficult years has been great. We see each other only a few days in every year, but the visits are something I look forward to, as a child looks forward to an afternoon at the circus."[46] He spent the first several months after Katherine's death writing personal responses to hundreds of friends, acquaintances, and strangers who had sent letters of condolence.

At the age of eighty-three, White wrote a new introduction to *One Man's Meat*, his collection of essays from *Harper's*

Magazine. In it, he gave readers a small picture of what his life was like after Katharine's death:

> The saltwater farm that served as the setting for this most tumultuous episode in my life has seen many changes in forty years. The sheep have disappeared, along with several other accessories. The elms have disappeared. I am still visible, pottering about, overseeing the incubations, occasionally writing a new introduction for an old book. I do the Sunday chores. I stoke the stove. I listen for the runaway toilet. I true up the restless rug. I save the whale. I wind the clock. I talk to myself.[47]

White continued to perform the routine chores of the farm as long as he was physically able and to take the canoe out onto the peaceful serenity of the lake as he had done all of his life. But he also had to rely on the help of housekeepers and extra farm hands to keep things running smoothly. In the last year of his life, White spent much time resting and spending time with his son Joel. Eventually, White grew too tired and weak to do much more than remain in bed. Joel would visit him and read from White's favorite book, *Walden*, or one of Thurber's humorous pieces.

Over the years, White's memory had begun to fail him. He'd read the daily newspaper, take a short nap, and then find himself searching for the paper again, having forgotten that he already read it. White's doctor diagnosed him with Alzheimer's disease, a brain disease that causes memory loss and dementia.

White died at the age of eighty-six in October 1, 1985. His family held a memorial service on October 26 at Blue Hill Congregational Church. On the church program, they reprinted the poem "Natural History," which White had written for Katharine many years earlier, soon after their marriage. He sent Katharine the poem from the King Edward Hotel in Toronto on November 30, 1929:

> The spider, dropping down from twig,
> Unwinds a thread of his devising:
> A thin, premeditated rig
> To use in rising.
>
> And all the journey down through space,
> In cool descent and loyal-hearted,
> He builds a ladder to the place
> From which he started.
>
> Thus I, gone forth, as spiders do,
> In spider's web a truth discerning,
> Attach one silken strand to you
> For my returning.[48]

There were two small messages on the bottom of the funeral service notice, both revealing important aspects of White's personality. "Everyone is welcome" and "Please, no flowers." His family knew that White would have felt sorry that any part of nature, even the flowers normally given to a grieving family, should have to suffer for him. He would have preferred that the flowers would live on.

Although, because of the enormous success of *Stuart Little*, *Charlotte's Web*, and *The Trumpet of the Swan*, White is perhaps first remembered as an author of children's books, the literary world recognized him as one of America's finest essayists. In his lifetime, he published over sixteen books and hundreds of essays. In fact, White sometimes felt puzzled at being labeled a children's writer. Still, he acknowledged that he did see the world from a child's point of view at times, being able to express the same wonder and curiosity about the way things worked. He felt that adults often don't recognize that children need to know why things happen the way they do. When he wrote his children's books, White maintained a true respect for his readers; he never wrote condescendingly or tried to shield them from the world. In 1938, he wrote an essay called "Children's Books," in which he explained his perspective on writing for a younger audience. The inspiration for the essay came from being surrounded on all sides by review copies of new children's books, some two hundred of them, taking up space on the chairs, beds, kitchen cabinet, under a sofa cushion, and lodged in his favorite armchair:

> Much of our adult morality, in books and out of them, has a stuffiness unworthy of the childhood. Our grown-up conclusions often rest on perilously soft bottoms. Try to tell a child even the simplest truths about planetary, cosmical, or spiritual things, and you hear strange echoes in your own head. "Can this be me?" a voice keeps asking, "can this be me?" Dozens of times, I have caught myself telling my boy things I didn't thoroughly comprehend myself, urging him toward conventional attitudes of mind and spirit I only half believed in and would myself gladly chuck overboard.[49]

But whether he penned a book about a boy who looked an awful lot like a mouse, a humorous essay on dog training, or a memoir about his childhood days at Belgrade Lake, E.B. White's central purpose for writing remained the same. "All I hope to say in books, all that I ever hope to say, is that I love the world."

1 White, E.B. *One Man's Meat.* New York: Harper & Brothers, 1942, pp. 201–202.

2 Plimpton, George A., and Frank H. Crowther. "The Art of the Essay, I: E.B. White," *The Paris Review*, no. 48 (Fall 1969), pp. 67–68.

3 "A Boy I Knew," *The Reader's Digest*, vol. 36, no. 218 (June 1940), pp. 33–36.

4 *Letters of E.B. White.* Edited by Dorothy Lobrano Guth. New York: Harper and Row, 1976, pp. 8, 9–10.

5 *One Man's Meat*, pp. 198–199.

6 White, E.B. *Second Tree from the Corner.* New York: Harper and Row, 1981, pp. 17–18.

7 *Letters of E.B. White*, p. 10

8 *One Man's Meat*, p. 88.

9 Strunk, William, Jr., and E.B. White. *The Elements of Style*, 3rd edition. New York: Macmillian, 1979, p. xiii.

10 Anderson, A.J. *E.B. White.* New Jersey: Scarecrow Press, 1978, p. 62.

11 *Letters of E.B. White*, pp. 62–63.

12 *Second Tree from the Corner*, p. 216.

13 White, E.B. *Essays of E.B. White.* New York: Harper & Row, 1977, p. 121.

14 *Letters of E.B. White*, p. 88–89.

15 E.B.W. to Joel White, December 31, 1930.

16 *One Man's Meat*, pp. 127–28.

17 E.B.W. to Stanley White, June 13, 1936.

18 White, E.B., and Katharine White. *A Subtreasury of American Humor*, London: Telegraph Books, 1988, pp. xvi, 517.

19 *One Man's Meat*, p. vii.

20 *Letters of E.B. White*, p. 512.

21 "The Librarian Said it was Bad for Children," *New York Times*, March, 1966, sec. X, p. 19.

22 *Letters of E.B. White*, p. 193.

23 *Letters of E.B. White*, p. 270.

24 *Letters of E.B. White*, pp. 651–652.

25 *Letters of E.B. White*, p. 375.

26 "Pigs and Spiders," *McClurg's Book News*, January 1953, p. 49.

27 Welty, Eudora. *The Eye of the Story*. New York: Vintage Books, 1979, p. 205.

28 *Letters of E.B. White*, pp. 397–98.

29 *Letters of E.B. White*, p. 409.

30 *Letters of E.B. White*, 455.

31 *Letters of E.B. White*, p. 449.

32 *Letters of E.B. White*, pp. 405–406.

33 "Krushchev and I (A Study in Similarities)," *The New Yorker*, September 26, 1959.

34 "James Thurber," *The New Yorker*, November 11, 1961.

35 *Letters of E.B. White*, p. 605.

36 *Letters of E.B. White*, p. 567.

37 *Letters of E.B. White*, p. 591.

38 Updike, John. *The New York Times Book Review*, June 1970, pp. 4–5.

39 *Letters of E.B. White*, p. 612.

40 *Letters of E.B. White*, p. 629.

41 *Letters of E.B. White*, p. 654.

42 E.B.W. to S.J. Perelman, August 1977.

43 Elledge, Scott. *E.B. White: A Biography*, p. 354.

44 *Katharine and E.B. White: An Affectionate Memoir*, Isabel Russell, p. 196.

45 White, Katharine S. *Onward and Upward in the Garden*. New York: Farrar, Straus, and Giroux, 1979, p. xix.

46 *E.B. White*, p. 356.

47 *One Man's Meat*, p. xiii.

48 *Letters of E.B. White*, p. 173.

49 *One Man's Meat*, p. 23.

1899   Elwyn Brooks White is born on July 17 in Mount Vernon, New York.

1913–1917   Student at Mount Vernon High School, where he publishes in the high school newspaper, *The Oracle*.

1920–1921   Works as editor-in-chief for Cornell University's *Daily Sun*.

1921   Graduates with a Bachelor of Arts from Cornell University.

1922   Travels across the country in a Model-T Ford, nicknamed "Hotspur," with his friend Howard Cushman for several months.

1922–1923   Wrote for the *Seattle Times* and took a trip to Alaska on the *S.S. Buford*, both as passenger and then as a steward.

1923–1924   Moves into a small apartment in Manhattan with three other Cornell graduates. Works for Frank Seaman, Inc. as a production assistant and advertising copywriter.

1925   Job at advertising firm for J.H. Newmaker. First essay appears in *The New Yorker*.

1927–1938   Begins to write regularly for *The New Yorker*.

1928   *Is Sex Necessary?*, a spoof on the present-day relationship manuals, appears, co-written with fellow *New Yorker* friend and cartoonist James Thurber. Also publishes a book of poems called *The Lady Is Cold*.

1929   Marries Katherine Sergeant Angell on November 13.

1930   On December 21, Katherine gives birth to their son Joel McCoun White.

1931–1934   Publishes *Ho-Hum: Newsbreaks from The New Yorker* (1931), *Another Ho-Hum* (1932), and *Every Day is Saturday* (1934).

1936   Publishes *Farewell to Model T* with Richard Lee Strout.

1938   *The Fox of Peapack* is released. White moves to North Brooklin, Maine, and begins writing a column for *Harper's Magazine* called "One Man's Meat."

1939   *Quo Vadimus or The Case for the Bicycle* is published.

1941   He and Katherine publish a compilation of American humorists called *A Subtreasury of American Humor*.

1942   *One Man's Meat*, a collection of his best pieces from *Harper's Magazine*, hits bookstores.

1944 White and Katherine move back to New York City.

1945 White releases *Stuart Little*, his first, and very popular, book written primarily for children.

1946 *The Wild Flag* is published.

1948 Awarded honorary degrees from University of Maine, Yale University, and Dartmouth College.

1949 Publishes *Here Is New York*.

1952 Second children's book, *Charlotte's Web*, is published.

1954 *The Second Tree from the Corner* is published.

1957 Decides to leave Manhattan to live at the farm in Maine.

1959 Revises and composes the introduction to the writing manual used by his former professor at Cornell University, William Strunk, Jr., and calls it *The Elements of Style*.

1960 The National Institute of Arts and Letters awards him the Gold Medal for Essays and Criticism.

1962 Publishes *The Points of My Compass*.

1963 Awarded Presidential Medal for Freedom by John F. Kennedy.

1970 *The Trumpet of the Swan*, White's third and last children's book, is published. Winner of the Laura Ingalls Wilder Medal for the overall contributions he made to children's literature.

1971 Winner of the National Medal for Literature.

1973 Given the Sequoyah Award and William Allen White Award for *The Trumpet of the Swan*. Also awarded American Academy of Arts and Letters. The cartoon feature of *Charlotte's Web* appears in theaters.

1976 *The Letters of E.B. White* is published.

1977 Katharine White dies.

1978 Awarded a Pulitzer Prize special citation in acknowledgment of his body of work.

1985 Dies on October 1 in North Brooklin, Maine.

STUART LITTLE

The Little family of Manhattan is pleased when their second son, Stuart, arrives, all two inches of him. Though he looks very much like a mouse, Stuart behaves like a boy. He is a fastidious dresser, an excellent sailor, and a brave adventurer. His small size allows him to do things regular-sized boys cannot, such as fish lost objects out of the drain, fetch Ping-Pong balls, and pull up stuck piano keys. But his size can also get him in trouble. The book follows Stuart Little through his adventures inside his New York City apartment, in Central Park, and finally out on the open road when he leaves home in search of his beloved, the lovely bird Margalo.

CHARLOTTE'S WEB

Wilbur arrives on the Arable farm as the smallest pig in the litter. He is about to be put to death because of his size when eight-year-old Fern Arable rescues him. She bottle feeds Wilbur until he's too big for the house and eventually Wilbur is sent to her uncle's farm, where Fern visits him every day after school. At first, Wilbur is lonely without Fern, but eventually he makes friends with the soft-voiced and generous-hearted Charlotte A. Cavatica, a friendly barn spider who lives in a web above his pen. A true friendship grows between Wilbur and Charlotte, and Charlotte shows herself to be a character of great ingenuity, particularly when it comes to saving Wilbur's life.

THE TRUMPET OF THE SWAN

Louis, a beautiful young trumpeter swan, is devastated to learn that he is different from the other swans: he has no ability to make the "Ko-hoh" mating call. Because of this handicap, he fears he will never earn the attention of Serena, another trumpeter swan with whom he has fallen in love. His human friend, Sam Beaver, and the Beaver family remain determined to help Louis. His own father steals a trumpet for Louis and hires a music teacher to help him learn to play. Louis catches on immediately and sets out on a journey to earn money playing music to help pay back the store for the stolen instrument.

1928 *The Lady is Cold*

1931 *Ho-Hum: Newsbreaks from* The New Yorker

1932 *Another Ho-Hum*

1934 *Every Day is Saturday*

1938 *The Fox of Peapack*

1939 *Quo Vadimus or the Case for the Bicycle*

1941 *A Subtreasury of American Humor*

1942 *One Man's Meat*

1945 *Stuart Little*

1946 *The Wild Flag*

1949 *Here is New York*

1952 *Charlotte's Web*

1954 *The Second Tree from the Corner*

1959 *The Elements of Style* (with William Strunk, Jr.)

1962 *The Points of My Compass*

1966 *E.B. White Reader*

1970 *The Trumpet of the Swan*

1976 *The Letters of E.B. White*

1977 *The Essays of E.B. White*

1981 *The Poems and Sketches of E.B. White*

1990 *Writings from* The New Yorker *1925–1976*

1999 *Salutations! Wit and Wisdom from* Charlotte's Web

Agosta, Lucien L. *E.B. White: The Children's Books*. New York: Twayne, 1995.

Elledge, Scott. *E.B. White*. New York: W.W. Norton & Company, 1984.

Sampson, Edward C. *E.B. White*. New York: Twayne, 1974.

Root, Robert L., ed. *Critical Essays on E.B. White*. New York: G.K. Hall, 1994.

White, E.B. *Charlotte's Web*. New York: Harper and Brothers, 1952.

———. *Letters of E.B. White*. Edited by Dorothy Lobrano Guth. New York: Harper and Row, 1976.

———. *Second Tree from the Corner*. New York: Harper and Row, 1981.

———. *Stuart Little*. New York: Harper and Row, 1973.

———. *The Trumpet of the Swan*. New York: Harper and Row, 1970.

Anderson, A.J. *E.B. White*. New Jersey: Scarecrow Press, 1978.

Angell, Roger. "E.B. White." Talk of the Town. *New Yorker* (October 14, 1985): 31.

Berg, Julie. *E.B. White*. Edina, Minn.: Abdo & Daughters, 1994.

Collins, David R. *To the Point: A Story about E.B. White*. Illustrations by Amy Johnson. Minneapolis: Carolrhoda Books, 1989.

Gherman, Beverly. *E.B. White, Some Writer!: A Biography*. 1st Beech Tree ed. New York: Beech Tree Books, 1994.

Gill, Brendan. *Here at the New Yorker*. New York: Random House, 1975.

Griffith, John W. *Charlotte's Web: A Pig's Salvation*. New York: Twayne, 1993.

Hall, Donald. "E.B. White on the Exercycle." *The National Review*, 29 (June 10, 1977): 671–72.

Hasley, Louis. "The Talk of the Town and the Country: E.B. White," *Connecticut Review*, 5 (October 1971): 37–45.

Kramer, Dale. *Ross and the New Yorker*. Garden City: Doubleday, 1951.

Neumeyer, Peter F. "E.B. White: Aspects of Style." *Horn Book Magazine*, v. 63, n. 5 (Sept–Oct 1987): 586–91.

Russell, Isabel. *Katharine and E.B. White: An Affectionate Memoir*. New York: W.W. Norton, 1988.

Singer, Dorothy G. "Charlotte's Web and Erikson's Life Cycle." *School Library Journal*, v. 22, n. 3 (Nov. 1975): 17–19.

Sale, Roger. *Fairy Tales and After: From Snow White to E.B. White*. Cambridge: Harvard University Press, 1978, pp. 258–67.

Thurber, James. "E.B.W." *Saturday Review* (October 15, 1938): 8–9.

Tingum, Janice. *E.B. White: The Elements of a Writer*. Minneapolis: Lerner, 1995.

Ward, S. (Stasia) *Meet E.B. White*. 1st ed. New York: PowerKids Press, 2001.

White, E.B. *Poems and Sketches of E.B. White*. New York: HarperCollins, 1983.

White, Katharine S. *Onward and Upward in the Garden*. New York: Farrar, Straus, and Giroux, 1979.

http://www.harperchildrens.com/authorintro/index.asp?authorid=10499
  [E.B. White Official home page]

http://www.webenglishteacher.com/white.html
  [Web English teacher, E.B. White)]

http://www.newyorker.com/
  [The New Yorker *magazine homepage]*

http://www.bartleby.com/141/
  [Online version of The Elements of Style*]*

AIMEE LABRIE graduated from Penn State with an MFA in fiction. Her short stories have appeared in *The Minnesota Review*, *Beloit Fiction Review*, *Pleiades*, *Iron Horse Literary Review*, and other literary journals. Last year, her short story collection placed as a finalist for the Sandstone Prize. She currently works as a publications manager in Philadelphia.